STARTING A
BUSINESS 101

FROM **CREATING A BUSINESS PLAN** AND **STICKING TO
A BUDGET** TO **MARKETING** AND **MAKING A PROFIT,**
YOUR ESSENTIAL PRIMER TO **STARTING A BUSINESS**

Michele Cagan, CPA

Adams Media

New York   London   Toronto   Sydney   New Delhi

Adams Media
An Imprint of Simon & Schuster, Inc.
100 Technology Center Drive
Stoughton, Massachusetts 02072

Copyright © 2023 by Simon & Schuster, Inc.

First Adams Media hardcover edition December 2023

ADAMS MEDIA and colophon are registered trademarks of Simon & Schuster, Inc.

For information about special discounts for bulk purchases, please contact Simon & Schuster Special Sales at 1-866-506-1949 or business@simonandschuster.com.

The Simon & Schuster Speakers Bureau can bring authors to your live event. For more information or to book an event, contact the Simon & Schuster Speakers Bureau at 1-866-248-3049 or visit our website at www.simonspeakers.com.

Manufactured in the United States of America

2 2024

Library of Congress Control Number: 2023944596

ISBN 978-1-5072-2122-8
ISBN 978-1-5072-2123-5 (ebook)

CONTENTS

INTRODUCTION 5

INTRODUCTION

If you've always dreamed of starting your own business, this book will help you succeed. From analyzing your potential business's competition to attracting investors to protecting your intellectual property, getting a business up and running can be a lot of work. In fact, millions of people try to launch new companies every year, and many of those new businesses end in failure. However, while it may be difficult, owning your own business can be financially and personally rewarding too. And being prepared may be the key to your business's success. By following the steps outlined in this book and planning carefully for success, you'll be able to create a business that grows sustainably, provides steady income, and builds a legacy for your family and your future.

In *Starting a Business 101*, you'll learn how to build a business from the ground up. You'll soon understand how to:

- Choose the right business for you.
- Create a winning business plan.
- Figure out the best source of financing.
- Determine optimal pricing for your products and services.
- Hire employees and contractors.
- Attract and retain your ideal customers.
- Keep track of your books and plan for taxes.
- Maintain a healthy work-life balance.
- And more.

With each lesson you learn, you'll be closer to success. Plus, having your own business gives you freedom and control over your livelihood. Once you take the plunge, you'll be excited, exhausted, frustrated, and empowered. At times it will be scary knowing that your current and future finances depend on the health of your business. That can also be a comfort, as you'll learn how to adapt and balance your finances, both of which can provide security in times of economic uncertainty. If you've taken the time to create a sturdy foundation that allows for sensible growth, you can be confident that your business will provide for you for many years to come.

Ultimately, though it's difficult knowing that the success of your business rests on your shoulders, each lesson in this book will give you a boost over your closest competition. You'll learn how to handle issues like negative cash flow, problem employees, late-paying customers, and will reap the rewards of being your own boss. No matter what type of business you choose to start, *Starting a Business 101* will help you overcome challenges, mitigate risk, and set your company on a path toward profitability. So, turn the page and let's begin.

Chapter 1

From an Idea to a New Business

You probably have business ideas all the time, but it takes more than an idea to launch a successful company. You'll need a heap of self-motivation, time, sweat, research, and focus to nurture your idea seed into a full-grown, profitable business. Because that's the dream—being your own boss, taking charge, and turning your passion into positive cash flow. That's the draw of entrepreneurship, and to live that dream you'll need to buckle up and buckle down to build your business.

You must choose the right business for you, even if that ends up looking differently than you had imagined. Your idea can be transformed by using a combination of your passion, strongest skills, available time and resources, and connections. You'll need to make sure that there are people who want to buy what you're selling. Chances are good that you'll have a customer base, but you'll need to find them and learn how to communicate in ways that will resonate with them. You'll need to track down and learn everything you can about your competitors, borrowing from their successes and carefully avoiding their failures. All of this effort will help you build the successful, profitable, sustainable business you've always wanted.

KNOW WHAT IT TAKES TO START A BUSINESS

Getting Your Ducks in a Row

It takes more than a good idea and a great attitude to start and maintain a business. While it may seem like you can post profits from the jump, virtually all "overnight" success stories were years in the making. It takes time to create, build, and grow a business—not to mention money, energy, patience, and support. With those resources, you'll be able to see your idea turn into a sustainable and profitable business. Just know that the road to starting your own business is a long and difficult one, so plan ahead.

There's a lot of misinformation online about starting a business. Social media makes it seem like this venture requires minimal time and effort for huge returns and endless tax write-offs. To be crystal clear, starting a business won't:

- Turn you into an overnight millionaire.
- Make all of your expenses tax-deductible.
- Protect you against personal responsibility lawsuits (or lawsuits where you are sued for your actions as an individual).
- Attract plenty of investors wanting to support you.
- Free up more time for your personal life.

No matter what you've seen online, creating and running a business takes a lot of hard work. Your business won't be hugely profitable in the first thirty days and won't be able to support you completely within months. And while business expenses will be deductible on your tax return, personal expenses still won't be.

THE TIME FACTOR

Small business owners work hard, and they work a lot. In fact, many surveys show that entrepreneurs work more than full-time employees, sometimes twice as much or more. One poll from the New York Enterprise Report found that 33% of entrepreneurs reported working at least fifty hours a week. Plus, 25% of those 33% of business owners reported working over sixty hours per week. That's why so many small business owners burn out. Focusing so much time on building your business leaves little time for relationships, health, rest, and fun.

With all of the time you'll be spending on your business, time management skills are crucial for your success. You'll be juggling your business, your home life, and possibly another job. It takes superb multitasking abilities and discipline to manage all of this successfully for the years it may take to start your business. You'll also need to have strong support systems in place when you just can't get everything done on your own.

THE MONEY FACTOR

Every business needs sufficient start-up funds. If your business idea requires inventory, machinery, equipment, and premises, your initial costs will be much greater than a company that can be started with a laptop. In addition, if you can't run your business without employees, your costs will also be higher than a solo venture. But even companies with very lean start-up budgets need funding, and it's often more than they expect.

Most small businesses won't produce profits for *at least* six months to a year, sometimes longer. That means every dime that comes in the door goes right back out. And, often, more money will be flowing out than in for quite a while. Remember, if this business will be your primary personal income source, all of your personal expenses factor into this cash flow equation. That means until or unless you get external business financing, you may personally end up borrowing a lot of money through loans and credit cards. Many business owners struggle with mounting debt, which can be difficult to overcome in the beginning stages. That's why it's crucial to make sure you have enough funding available.

THE TAX FACTOR

Many new entrepreneurs are under the incorrect impression that they'll be able to run a profitable business that generates huge tax savings. They expect to be able to run all of their expenses through the business, writing off even their personal expenses. This sadly isn't true, which often comes as a shock on the first tax return.

When a business generates profits, it also generates a tax bill from the federal and state governments. Who pays those taxes—you or your business—depends on how the business is set up. But for the majority of small business start-ups, the business income flows through to the business owner's tax return, and the owner bears the responsibility for reporting and paying the taxes. Having an LLC, a limited liability company, as your legal business structure doesn't affect this at all. LLCs don't exist for tax purposes—they are legal structures.

As for personal expenses, some (or a portion of some) of those will become legitimate business expenses. These legitimate expenses are mainly for mixed-use, such as your personal phone or car that you also use for the business. The business portion of these expenses then becomes deductible. But things like meals eaten while you're working (not during an in-person meeting with other people), clothes that you bought for a personal photo shoot, or your at-home subscriptions don't magically become deductible when you start a business.

THE SUCCESS FACTOR

More than five million new businesses were started in the US in 2022. Approximately 10% of those failed within the first year, and another 70% will likely fail within the first 2–5 years. That doesn't mean you should be discouraged. It gives you the opportunity to look at what went wrong for other businesses so yours can avoid the same fate. The most common causes for business failure include:

- Lack of planning
- Running out of money
- Poor management
- Inability to adapt to changing conditions
- Ineffective marketing

Each of these can be overcome with solid planning and flexibility. No matter how good your plan is, reality will throw you a curveball. That's why your business has to be able to adjust to whatever is happening in the world in order to survive.

A One-Month Snapshot of Start-Ups

According to the US Census Bureau, 418,904 new businesses started in November 2022. The majority of those—191,226—were formed in the Southern US. Only 48,850 of those new companies nationwide planned to pay employee wages. The top start-up industries that month included construction, retail, professional services, and administrative and support services.

CHOOSING THE RIGHT BUSINESS FOR YOU

What Do You Want to Do?

When it comes to choosing the best business for you to start, there are many factors to take into consideration. As you're trying to decide what to do, think about:

- **Passion.** How much do you care about the business you're considering?
- **Skill set.** What do you already know how to do well?
- **Industry expertise.** What knowledge and experience can you bring to the business?
- **Motivation.** Do you have the ability to get things done even when you don't want to?
- **Runway.** How much cash can you contribute, raise, or borrow to fund your business while it's in the start-up phase?
- **Budget.** How much money do you expect to spend on the business until it's viable, and what do you plan to spend it on?
- **Scalability.** Do you have the capacity to meet increasing demand or workload?
- **Demand.** Will people or businesses want to buy what you're selling?
- **Market saturation.** How many other businesses are selling what you plan to sell?

Give yourself time and really think about the factors in relation to your personal interests, goals, and experience. Your business idea should score high on all—or at least most—of these factors. If it doesn't, you might want to consider starting a different type of business. For example, a company you're passionate about and have a high level of expertise in won't be successful if there's no demand for what you plan to sell, or if the market is already oversaturated. At the same time, selling a product that's in high demand with lots of room for growth when you have no interest in it and hate working on it can also lead to business failure. Strive for a balance between your passion and knowledge and the market allowance.

Perfect Is the Enemy of Done

No business idea will score perfectly in every factor category. As you're pondering what business you'd like to start, don't aim for a perfect outcome. Instead, take your best idea—the one with the most potential—and get started. You'll make mistakes, hopefully ones you can recover from and fix. If you wait for everything to be perfect, you'll never launch.

TURN WHAT YOU LOVE INTO WHAT YOU DO

Passion projects can be fun and fulfilling, and turning them into a profitable business can satisfy both personal and professional goals. To start a business that you'll be passionate about, think about the things you love to do and rank them from favorite to least favorite. Once you have that list, you can start brainstorming about possible ways to transform a passion into a viable business prospect.

Your next step is making a list of all the things you know how to do, the skill set you'll bring to your fledgling company. Even if your passion and your current work don't seem to have anything in common, you can probably still find some overlap in skills you'll need. Include the skills you'd want to highlight on your resume, as well as the talents and abilities you would bring to the table. Examples of skills relevant to running a business include:

- Software and apps proficiency
- Editorial or copywriting experience
- Bookkeeping
- Data analysis
- Organization
- Time management
- Creativity
- Written and verbal communication
- Negotiation
- Research

In addition, make sure to list all of the skills necessary to create the products or provide the services you plan to sell, such as carpentry or acupuncture. These will be specific to this particular business, as opposed to the general business skills listed above.

WHAT YOU HAVE AND WHAT YOU NEED

Your next step will be to take an inventory of your resources. This list will include things like cash, credit lines, equipment, physical space, and other assets you already have on hand that can be used to launch your business. When you know what resources you have, you'll be able to determine what else you'll need to get your company started.

Once you've got your physical resources sorted, it's time to focus on your knowledge and experience. This is different than your skill set, or the things you can do. It's more about your industry knowledge and expertise, whether you gained that knowledge through a job, a volunteer program, or your life experience. These resources include things like knowing which suppliers deliver on time and offer beneficial payment terms, for example. You'll also want to include any licenses and certifications you've earned. Resources can also include your network of colleagues, contacts, and mentors.

THE EXTERNAL FACTORS

Once you've catalogued everything you can bring to the business, it's time to look at the market and see whether your business proposition has a chance. For your business to succeed, there needs to be demand for whatever you're selling, room for your business in the market, and the capacity to grow when (or even before) demand makes that necessary. You can learn about the first two—demand and market saturation—by conducting thorough market research.

Scalability can be a little harder to pin down. Your business will need the capacity to grow as demand grows, increasing efficiency and profitability. A business that depends 100% on you to perform services, for example, won't be scalable in terms of increased demand but can be scalable in terms of profitability. However, if you can bring on employees or partners to share that workload, you could make your business more scalable. Scaling too early or too late can lead to business failure, so it's important to listen closely to the demands of your client base.

CONDUCTING MARKET RESEARCH

Knowledge Is Power!

Before you launch a business, you'll need to make sure there's a pool of interested customers ready to buy whatever you're planning to sell. That pool of potential customers will be your market, and you'll need to find out as much as you can about them. Through extensive research, you'll learn a wealth of information about your future customers, including:

- Their demographic information.
- Their buying habits.
- What triggers their buying behavior.
- How they choose the products and services they use.
- What problems they're trying to solve.

With that information, you'll be able to create customer persona profiles. These profiles function as avatars that stand in for a particular segment of your target market. You'll understand what motivates a subset of your customers' purchases, what drives them to spend money, and what problem you can solve for them. Plus, you'll learn what entices them to buy from you instead of your competitors.

Of course, there's a price for that information, so you'll need to carve out space in your budget for things like marketing data, research assistance, and surveys. But this will be money well spent, as it will give you direct insights into your customer base and their buying habits.

What Are Demographics?

Demographics are statistics and facts that describe a particular population. They include things like age, location, marital status, gender, education level, and income. Gathering this information will help you get to know your core customers so you can speak to them to prompt a response.

WHY BOTHER WITH MARKET RESEARCH?

While you'll use your market research to help you define and communicate with your customer pool, you can also use it in other ways to help you launch your business. Solid market research can help you:

- Reach customers in the way customers prefer.
- Secure funding.
- Identify additional business opportunities (such as add-on products or services).
- Figure out where and how to advertise.
- Properly price your products.

Without market research, you'll be flying blind. With it, you'll have a stronger sense of whether your business can succeed before you launch. The bottom line is this: Market research can propel your new business toward success and help you avoid potential pitfalls.

FOUR WAYS TO GATHER MARKET DATA

If you've never done market research before, it can feel daunting. You're collecting information that will help you refine your ideas and pinpoint what your potential customers want. The best way to find out what they want is to ask them. To figure out what you want to ask, you can start by gathering general information that will help you narrow down your questions, allowing for the most valuable information to be given.

There are four main ways to conduct your market research:

1. Do secondary research: Gather existing information from a variety of sources, such as government databases, industry reports, and competitor websites.
2. Send out surveys: Create a set of questions and ask your target customers to answer them by reaching out through email or social media.
3. Conduct interviews: Reach out to your potential customers and talk to them one-on-one to find out how and why they use similar products or services.
4. Use focus groups: Gather a small group of people that demographically match your target audience and lead them through a group discussion centering on your product or service offering.

The first two methods generally won't cost much, if anything at all. For secondary research, you can find demographic information from the US Census Bureau at www.census.gov, industry data from the US Bureau of Labor Statistics at www.bls.gov, and the scoop on your competition by doing deep dives on their websites. You can send out online surveys using tools like Google Forms, SurveyMonkey (www.surveymonkey.com), or Wufoo (www.wufoo.com). Keep your questions short and to the point, and use different types of answer formats, such as multiple choice, response rating (like a 1–5 scale), or text boxes for open-ended answers.

For individual interview participants, you might offer gift cards, special discounts for your business, or samples of whatever you're selling in exchange for their time. These conversations can be done remotely or in person, and you'll want to record the session either way (just make sure you let the interviewee know that you're recording). Focus group participants normally expect to get paid, and if you've never hosted a focus group before, you might want to invest in a professional discussion leader to get reliable results.

CREATING YOUR CUSTOMER PERSONA PROFILES

Once you've collected your market research, you'll use the information to create your customer personas. When you know exactly who you're talking to, it's much easier to connect with them. It's also easier to avoid language or topics that would turn them off. For example, you wouldn't talk to first-time grandmothers with multiple pets in the same way you'd talk to young college students with fur allergies.

To create these avatars, start with demographic information. Knowing the basic facts will help you begin to see individuals inside the giant customer pool. Then you can begin to add in what you know about their lifestyles, buying preferences, needs, and concerns. Giving each avatar a name will help them come alive in your imagination and give you an edge when you're creating marketing content. It's easier to talk to a "real person" than to a vague collection of statistics.

ANALYZING THE COMPETITION

Know the Players, Know the Game

Understanding your competition before you launch your small business will dramatically shift the odds of success in your favor. You'll gain insights and information you won't find anywhere else, and that knowledge can help you avoid pitfalls, learn successful practices, and jump-start your company's growth. When learning about your competitors, you'll uncover both opportunities for success and threats to that success, and you'll sadly realize that there are probably more similar businesses that share your market.

All these key pieces of data will fall into place as you conduct a competitive analysis—an evaluation of the strengths and weaknesses of your chief competitors. From their products and services to their marketing messages, everything you learn here will give you an advantage as you get ready to launch.

WHY COMPETITIVE ANALYSIS MATTERS

Gaining a thorough understanding of your competitors will give your company an edge. You'll uncover important clues that will help you maximize the potential success of your business idea. In addition, having this information will help you figure out:

- Your company's unique selling proposition (USP), or what makes your product or service different from everyone else's.

- Strengths and weaknesses of your business relative to each competitor.
- Threats to your current and future success.
- Possible products or services to add in (now or in the future).
- Potential niches that aren't already oversaturated.

As you study your competitors, you'll see all the things they're doing successfully and use that a guide to further your business. You'll also see the things they aren't doing well, gaining insight from their mistakes or areas they've overlooked.

WHO ARE YOUR COMPETITORS?

Before you can begin to analyze your competitors, you have to know who they are. This will include direct, indirect, and replacement competitors, the last of which are especially tricky to identify. Direct competitors sell basically the same products and services that your company sells. You can find them by doing a simple search for whatever you're selling and see what comes up. You can then narrow that search by factors like physical location or price points. For example, if you're selling handmade ceramic mugs, you can do an online search for that and add descriptors like "under $50" or "near me."

Indirect competition covers products or services that aren't exactly the same, but can fall into the same general category. For example, a donut shop and a burger joint both offer different products, but they're both restaurant food, making them indirect competitors. Another example could be bookkeepers and virtual assistants who either provide or sub out bookkeeping services. Your indirect competitors will target the same general market as you, just in a different way.

Replacement competitors won't be in the same category but could satisfy the same basic need for the customer. An example could be frozen dinners replacing a restaurant chain, or DIY bookkeeping software for bookkeepers.

Competitor analysis will also include what rival businesses are selling and how their offerings compare to yours. You'll look at factors such as their pricing, target market, market share, marketing strategies, quality, suppliers, and more.

You may also be able to get some new ideas for upsell products or related services they offer that you haven't yet considered. This could help you brainstorm future growth opportunities for your company.

Upselling for Bigger Sales

Upselling is a marketing tool that encourages customers to add on to a purchase they're already making. Examples of common upsells include adding shrimp to a salad order, upgrading to business class when you book a flight, and gift wrapping a purchase. This is different than cross-selling, which encourages customers to buy products similar or complementary to their purchase.

HOW TO COLLECT COMPETITOR DATA

To keep your analysis consistent and organized, start by creating a spreadsheet or table that lists all the competitors you want to study (put this in column one) and the factors you want to look at (put this in row one). This will help you compare different competitors, get an industry snapshot, and help you identify key trends and strategies. Keep your grid flexible so you can add competitors and factors as you come across new information.

Start with basic background information on each company you've included so you can learn more about their businesses. This could include things like how long they've been in business, their main location (either physical or online), company size, other companies or brands they have partnered with, and why or how they built their business. You can find information like this on company websites, professional social media sites, and websites that have current or former employees' ratings of a business.

Next, try to get a sense of the customers they're actively targeting—who they're trying to talk to. You may have to look at their messaging, including their mission statement, their latest social media posts, and customer comments or reviews. Since they are your competitors, it's likely they're targeting the same audience you are, though their messaging may be directed toward slightly different customer subsets. By looking at their approach, you can more easily focus on your audience and messaging.

You may also want to try to find out what software and apps your competitors are using. Doing this research can help you identify tools that you'll be able to use in your business. You may be able to find out how competitors are invoicing, what customer relationship management (CRM) system they're using, their online sales platform, and more. Some of this information can be found by becoming a customer yourself—buying something from them, signing up for their mailing list, or contacting customer service to see what the processes are like.

IDENTIFY COMPETITOR SHORTFALLS

One of the best things you can learn from the competition is what they're doing wrong. Diving into that aspect of their businesses can help you avoid their mistakes and create a profitable niche. It may result in some of their customer base coming to you, which can help increase your market share more quickly. Some of their shortfalls may include:

- What their product or service is missing.
- Which customer group is underserved.
- Social media posts receiving little or no engagement.
- Bad reviews or complaints online.
- Problems using their website.
- Under- or overpriced products or services.

You can find a lot of this information through online searches, including doing deep dives on their websites, social media, and other channels they use to reach their target market. Paying attention to where your competitors fall short will provide valuable insights, allowing you to capitalize on areas they've missed while avoiding the mistakes they've made. Learning from a competitor's mistakes is invaluable.

FOCUSING YOUR IDEA

When Smaller Is Better

It's the trademark of an entrepreneur: dozens of ideas for businesses with new plans cropping up all the time. Chasing a handful of new ideas can feel exciting but rarely results in successful ventures. It's well worth your time to try to focus your ideas, whittling the dozens down into a few that could really work, and then narrowing those down to the one that has the best chance of success. But with so much passion flying around inside your head, it's hard to know where to start.

That's why your focus path will look more like a funnel than a trail. You'll keep narrowing the idea pool until you're left with a few truly viable businesses. Once you're down to a handful of potentially profitable ideas, you'll take a critical eye to each and make some preliminary assessments to figure out which has the best chance of success.

GET OUTSIDE INPUT

As you're focusing your business ideas, it pays to get some feedback from trusted friends and colleagues. They can help you tweak and perfect your idea, or they can let you know if it's unlikely to work. Input will be especially helpful if you consult with people who fit into the target market you're aiming for.

For the best results here, you'll want to ask everyone the same questions. Remember, you might not get the answers you want, but that can help you move away from an idea that doesn't have much traction. It's easy to fall in love with your business ideas and see them through only that lens. Honest feedback here—positive or negative—provides important insights from a different perspective.

What should you ask? Start with the basics:

- Do you think this idea has potential for success?
- Would you buy the product or service? If not, why not?
- How much would you be willing to pay for it?
- Where are you getting this product or service, or something similar, now?
- How can I make this idea better?

Even if you don't have any acquaintances that fit your ideal customer profile, ask anyway. Objective people can still provide valuable feedback and possibly connect you with people who fit your target audience.

NARROW THE BUSINESS TYPE

There are many types of businesses you can start, but they all typically fall into basic categories based on what's being sold. The three main types are physical products, digital products, and services.

Businesses that sell physical products, such as paper plates, cars, dishwashers, and toys, cost more to start than companies that sell digital products or services. Physical products also cost more to modify and are harder to move or replace if they fall out of favor or have short shelf lives.

Businesses that sell digital products, such as ebooks, online courses, and worksheets, require a lot of lead time to create. Whatever item you're choosing to sell, you have to create the content before you can sell it.

Service businesses, such as tech support, cybersecurity, or legal, can be the fastest and cheapest to start but require the greatest ongoing time investment, especially if you personally provide the service. These businesses have a built-in hard limit of the amount you can sell, as you only have so much capacity to work in a day.

Choosing the business type you want to run can help direct the rest of your idea flow. If you know you don't want to sell products of any kind, that immediately narrows your options to service businesses, for example.

BALANCE YOUR SKILLS AND PASSIONS

Though we've talked about this overlap before, the best business ideas combine your passions with your existing business skill set. The trick is to figure out where these important factors overlap, which can help bring your business idea into sharper focus.

Start by listing ten to twelve business skills that you currently have honed. They can be from other jobs, courses you've taken, or general life experience that translates well for business management. Next, jot down ten to twelve things you feel excited about. This could be an industry, like graphic design or landscaping, a new trend you're following, or something you love to do, like drawing or hiking. Link any skills and passions that seem to go together or intersect. For example, a graphic design passion would link to skills like artistic ability and proficiency with design software. Focus your business idea where you see the greatest intersection of your skills and passions.

Find Your *Ikigai*

Ikigai, or "reason for being," is a Japanese concept that combines four important aspects of life: your mission (what the world needs), your passion (what you love), your vocation (what you do), and your profession (what you can get paid for). The idea of *ikigai* encourages you to find your purpose, one that will bring bliss.

PASSION OR PROFIT?

When you whittle your ideas down to one, it might not be the one you feel the most passionate about. At that point, you'll need to be honest with yourself about *why* you want to start the business. Your most desired business (your passion) may still be able to turn a profit, just not as well as other options might. If you really want to launch a passion project, as opposed to a critical income-earning venture, that will factor into your selection process as well.

If you're okay doing something you love while scraping out a meager profit, breaking even, or taking losses, pursuing your dreams may be fulfilling on many levels. Maybe you retired and want to create the business you've always dreamed about. Or maybe your business is starting out as a side gig where the outlet is more important than the income. Whatever your reasons, if following your passion is the number one factor for choosing a business idea, you still need to take all the business-building steps. That way, you'll be able to pursue it for years to come.

However, if profit is your driving force, you may need to set your passion aside, at least for now. You may have to move it to the back burner while you focus on building a successful business with the potential for sustainable growth and positive cash flow.

ASSESSING YOUR TIME AND RESOURCES

Count Your Chickens

Creating and running a business take more time, money, energy, and other resources than most new entrepreneurs realize. As you're fleshing out the type of company you're building, it's important to properly estimate the resources you'll need and properly account for what you already have. It's common for new business owners to underestimate what they'll need and overestimate what they have. You can avoid that trap by taking inventory of what you already have available and researching how much more it will take to get your business off the ground.

HOW MUCH TIME DO YOU REALLY HAVE?

Working for yourself takes a lot of willpower and self-motivation. No one else will be monitoring your time or work—it's all up to you. At the same time, your available time will be limited by the other obligations in your life. It's critical for you to honestly assess the amount of time you'll have available to devote to your business. Keep in mind that most small business owners work twice as much as employees, and a forty-hour work week is practically unheard of, especially during the start-up phase.

Take an inventory of your available time, making sure to include some downtime for yourself so you don't burn out before your company launches. Critically assess your work capacity (how fast you're able to get things done). For newly acquired skills, double the time you think it will take to complete tasks. Then map out all of the tasks that need to be done to both launch the business and keep it running for the first three months. Remember to include the following assets that your business may use: home office space, storage space and shelving, computers, printers, desks, phone(s), and vehicle(s).

Once you know how much time you'll need to complete all of your tasks and how much time you can devote to the business, you'll understand how long the starting phase will take. You will then have a realistic timeline to work with, and you can determine if you'll need additional help, whether in the form of employees, contractors, or partners. Hint: You *will* need extra help.

TAKING STOCK OF YOUR
AVAILABLE ASSETS

Your personal net worth will be a starting point for the assets you can bring to the business. While you may not use—or may not want to use—all of these assets, it's important to know what you have on hand. The easiest way to figure this out is by creating your own net worth statement, a worksheet that details what you have, what you owe, and what you own. It's sort of like a house: You have a house, you owe the balance of your mortgage, and you own whatever portion of the house is paid off. Net worth works the same way but with everything—your home, car, 401(k), credit card balances—included in the mix.

Keep in mind that some of these resources won't flow to your business intact. For example, taking money out of your 401(k) comes with an income tax hit plus possibly an extra 10% early withdrawal penalty. Taking a home equity loan or home equity line of credit (HELOC) comes with interest on top of the amount you borrow, and in most cases that interest will not be tax-deductible.

Most people start and end with cash, or assets they can quickly convert to cash, like stocks or other investments, and available credit. As you list assets that you could use in the business, don't forget:

- Home office space
- Storage space and shelving
- Computers
- Printers
- Desks
- Phone
- Vehicle

Once you know what you have to work with, you can determine how much money and what other assets you're able to contribute to the business. Some assets, like cash, will be fully contributed. Other assets, like a phone and laptop, might be shared with the business. Once you have an available assets inventory, you can figure out what you'll still need to obtain from other sources.

Remember that if you use your home equity or personal credit cards to fund your business, you will be on the hook to pay that money back. That's true whether your business succeeds or fails. So be cautious when using your personal credit as a business resource.

$3,000

According to the US Small Business Administration (SBA), you need about $3,000 to start a microbusiness. That's a company with no more than nine employees, including the business owners. They also estimate that it takes between $2,000 to $5,000 to start a home-based franchise.

ROUND UP YOUR EXTERNAL RESOURCES

Even though entrepreneurship is often a solo venture, that doesn't mean you can't turn to other people who can help you get started. Your contacts list is a great place to start when you're creating your list of external resources. This doesn't necessarily only mean people you could go to for loans. You may need help from:

- Mentors you can turn to for advice.
- Potential partners with complementary skill sets.
- Business contacts you can network with.
- Contacts who have relationships with banks.
- Friends who have access to properties and physical assets.
- Family members and friends who can lend you their time.
- Other acquaintances, who can refer customers to you.

If you want your business to succeed, connect with every possible contact you can. You never know where something key to your launch could come from or who might introduce you to just the person you need to keep things going.

FINDING THE RIGHT LOCATION

Setting Up Shop

Choosing the best spot for your new business takes thought and effort, whether your business will be at home or somewhere else. Your location sets the tone for your company and affects how customers and vendors interact with the business. Plus, it will impact how you feel about going to work every day.

Whether you're leaning toward running your business from home, a strip mall, or an office park, do some research before you make a commitment. You'll need to develop a strategy to help you figure out the right location. To do that, you'll need to consider seven important factors: business type, location needs, budget, your stakeholders, location amenities, saturation, and zoning laws. As you're looking for a location, remember, your business will be housed there for a long time. It's not easy to change locations, so make sure the place you choose is right for your business for the next few years.

BUSINESS TYPE

Your business likely fits into one of the following types, and this will dictate the type of space you'll need:

- **Solo service:** Freelancers, virtual assistants, home organizers, and other professions where you don't have in-person interaction with customers in your space. These are easily launched from home or coworking spaces.

- **Interactive service:** Therapists, tax preparers, and other professions where clients routinely come to your office. These may call for a more formal office setup to keep clients at ease.
- **Remote retail:** Online shops that sell goods. These may not need storefronts, but they will need space to house raw materials and finished products before they're sold.
- **In-person retail:** Bookstores, cafés, dispensaries, and other stores where customers shop in person. These will need physical spaces to sell goods, house products, and more.
- **Mobile retail:** Food trucks, pop-up shops, and other businesses that move from place to place. Aside from the changing location space, you may still need warehousing for storage.

LOCATION NEEDS

Do you know exactly what you need from your business location? Think about everything you plan to use the space for and how you can maximize the property's value for your company. You may need a small intimate office, a large office space with room for employees, a warehouse or other storage capacity, a storefront to house a retail shop, or a full kitchen with or without seating.

In addition, you want to think about the character of your location. Is it posh and trendy? Warm and welcoming? Bright and impersonal? The property you choose will reflect the personality of your business, and that in turn will attract a specific type of customer—preferably people in your target audience. Then make a list of all your needs and try to find a place that checks most of the boxes.

BUDGET

Your budget will play a huge part in determining your business location. Remember to consider more than just the rent or purchase price when you're looking at places. Along with rent, you may need to include additional costs, such as renovations, décor, utilities, taxes, and permits.

Additionally, it pays to look into economic incentives. State and local governments may offer tax breaks, grants, or other financial bonuses to businesses who choose to locate in specific areas.

Take Advantage of Incentives

Government incentive programs can help your new business stay afloat with special tax credits, grants, and other benefits. These incentives are often tied to things like creating jobs, improving energy efficiency, and redeveloping specific areas. You can find information about state and local incentive programs on their government websites.

YOUR STAKEHOLDERS

It's important to think beyond yourself when choosing a business location, even if you're the only one working there for now. Consider all of your potential stakeholders (the people who will be involved with your business), like customers, employees, suppliers, neighbors/community members, investors, lenders, and co-owners/partners.

Asking yourself some key questions will help you figure out if a prospective location could work for your stakeholders: Is it conveniently located for your target customers? Will vendors be able to make deliveries easily? Will employees be able to find parking and feel safe walking to and from work? Thinking about this now will help you steer clear of locations that your stakeholders may want to avoid.

LOCATION AMENITIES

While you're considering locations for your business, look into the available amenities. Those can have a direct impact on the potential success—or failure—of your company. You'll want to make it as easy as possible for customers to find and get to your place of business. If it's difficult for them to access, they'll find somewhere else to go. Look into:

- Parking, whether it's paid or free.
- Proximity to public transportation.
- Local restaurants for employees and customers to visit.
- Easy access accommodations (from ramps to handicap parking spots).
- Accessibility from main roads.
- Attractive, well-lit grounds.

Think about shops, mini-malls, and office buildings you've been to. You may not remember their benefits, but you probably remember what made them difficult to visit. Anything you didn't like about a previous shopping experience, your customers won't like either.

SATURATION

You want your business to be in a spot where your ideal customers tend to gather, but not within the same area as other competing businesses. For example, you might find a great spot for your coffee shop, but if there are three other coffee shops within a few blocks, that will divide your customer pool.

Look for a spot where there's enough demand for whatever you're selling but not so much supply that you'll struggle to get enough people in your door. In the best circumstances, the other businesses right near you will be complementary, selling different products to the same target customer so they're likely to stop by while they're in the area.

ZONING LAWS

Zoning laws dictate where your business can operate, and they're not always straightforward. That's particularly true when it comes to running a business out of your home, so you'll want to make sure you know what's allowed and what isn't. You can find information about zoning laws at your local (city or county) department of planning or a similar department.

Whether you own or rent your business space, local zoning laws apply. Areas are generally zoned as either commercial or residential. Even inside commercial zones, some types of businesses may be banned or restricted. Zoning laws can also dictate the number of parking spaces available to your business, acceptable hours of operation, and how big your sign can be.

Home-based businesses that are generally allowed by zoning rules may restrict the number of customers allowed on the premises at any one time or the number of visitors to the premises on any day. If you live in a condominium or belong to a homeowner's association, you may be subjected to stricter-than-local zoning laws. Make sure to check any covenants that come with your property. Renters should also make sure their leases don't explicitly forbid home-based businesses.

Chapter 2

The Building Blocks of Business

Your business needs a firm foundation to launch from. Without that, it can't become profitable, enjoy sustainable growth, or provide you with a reliable income. In these early stages, the more care you put into building your business, the more you'll get out of it over time. Some of the decisions you'll make during this stage will have lasting effects for the company, such as business structure and funding sources. Many small businesses fail because they gloss over the early planning stage, making mistakes that they can't fix after the fact. Your business will avoid these problems as you take the time and effort to build that steady foundation.

One of the most critical early issues involves funding: how much money you'll need, where to find it, and how to secure it. Whether you go the bootstrap route, pitch to investors, or try to borrow from the bank, you have to start with solid numbers and realistic projections. You'll need to know how long your business's money should last and how soon you expect the business to be self-supporting. Figuring all of this out and putting it all together will help you set a solid foundation to grow your business on.

CREATING A BUSINESS PLAN

Mapping It Out

It may be the most important ingredient to small business success, but most budding entrepreneurs don't bother with business plans. The lack of planning comes from myths about business plans that don't ring true, at least not anymore. Some of the biggest misconceptions about business plans include:

- **They must run about fifty pages long.** Not true. Your business plan can be a one-pager, called a lean plan, or a robust document running around fifteen to twenty pages.
- **Only established businesses need business plans.** Not true. Creating a business plan at the outset helps you build and grow your business effectively and successfully.
- **You can't change the plan once you have shared it.** Not true. A business plan can and should change whenever you need it to.
- **It's too hard to write one.** Not true. Well, a little true, but it's not nearly as hard as you think it will be, especially if you follow the free SBA business plan template (www.sba.gov).
- **You won't really use it.** Not true. A business plan can help you attract investors, get funding, and set a clear path for you to take toward success.

There is no wrong way to create a business plan, as long as it works for you and does what you need. Even a one-page lean start-up business plan will provide guidance and structure to your business and help you take the steps you need for your business to succeed.

FOUR SURPRISING WAYS A BUSINESS PLAN CAN HELP

The most pressing reason to create a business plan is to obtain funding. But that's far from the only way a business plan can help you succeed. Here are four ways your business plan can make starting your company easier:

1. **It will help you set and meet goals.** How will you know if your business is succeeding? When you compare it against your plan, it's reaching predetermined milestones. If those milestones haven't been set, you won't be able to tell where you are along the road to success. Your business plan provides a framework for achievement.

2. **It will help you avoid mistakes that will hurt your business.** As you're creating your plan, you'll be able to identify potential pitfalls—like running out of cash or supply chain issues—before they happen and figure out ways to avoid or overcome them.

3. **It will help you make crucial decisions.** Starting your own business involves thousands of decisions, and some of those can spell life or death for your venture. Creating a business plan lets you run through scenarios and consider tough questions ahead of time, so you can make the best possible choices.

4. **It will help speed up your success.** Research shows that companies that use business plans grow up to 30% faster than those with no plans.

WHAT GOES INTO A BUSINESS PLAN?

A solid business plan, even if it's short, hits all the major points that will affect your business. There's a sort of standard order, mainly based on what banks look for when considering loans, but you don't have to follow that if it doesn't suit your business's needs. Still, you'll want your business plan to include:

- Executive summary: An introduction and bird's-eye view of your company, usually written last even though it comes first in the plan.
- Company description: General information about the business you're starting, including top-level information about what you'll be selling, your customers/clients, the company's legal structure, and your primary business location.
- Market analysis: Detailed information about your ideal target customers, including demographics, customer problems, and how those problems are currently being solved.
- Competitor analysis: Assessment of the competition, including their strengths and weaknesses, the advantages they have, and what sets your business apart from them.
- Marketing plan: Information about your proposed pricing, advertising activities, and sales strategy.
- Management team and key personnel: An introduction to the people who will be managing various aspects of your business, whether they'll be internal or external, and special skills and experience they bring to the business.
- Sale and expense projections and other key financial information: A realistic estimate of one to five years of expected expenses and revenues, existing start-up capital, and a break-even analysis.

When you're creating the plan for yourself, it can be as short or long as you want it. You can add to it over time, change it when challenges or unexpected issues crop up, and include whatever information is most useful for you. When you're using the plan to get a loan or attract investors, you should take a more professional, polished approach that includes a higher level of detail than your personal framework plan.

USING YOUR PLAN TO GET FINANCING

Business plans can be used as tools to help you get outside funding for your start-up. Your audience will likely form their first impression of your company based on its plan, so you'll want it to look perfect and contain the exact information they're asking for.

Appearances matter here, and your plan should be designed and laid out to impress. It should be well organized and logical. If the lender asks for a specific format, use it. And before you submit the plan, proofread it—better yet, have someone else proof it for you—to make sure there are no spelling or grammar mistakes.

You'll also want to have a killer executive summary that's clear and compelling. If the person receiving your business plan isn't impressed, they won't keep reading and your plan will go in the "no" pile. Your executive summary should create interest and excitement while providing just enough information for the reader to keep going.

Keep It Real

Don't oversell your start-up in the business plan. Avoid hype and excessive language like "hottest," "best," and "groundbreaking." Don't overestimate potential revenues and underplay costs. Instead, win your audience over with compelling data and realistic projections.

PERFECTING YOUR PITCH DECK

Persuade and Prosper

Pitch decks are short presentations that businesses can use to attract customers, talent, and most often investors. These decks are typically created digitally in a slideshow format and will be a summary of the highlights of your business plan, laid out in a way that sparks interest and excitement. After all, the immediate goal of your pitch deck is to get a call back, a next meeting, or a request for additional information.

For most small business owners, a strong pitch deck is the key to unlocking investor funds. So, your pitch needs to be unique, compelling, and unforgettable. Though that sounds intimidating, just take the time to get it right. Get feedback from mentors, colleagues, and potential investors that didn't bite. This is your company's first impression, so it's critical to make it a great one!

WHAT TO INCLUDE IN YOUR DECK

Your pitch deck should pull from your business plan in an extremely pared-down form, laid out in a way that builds interest. A deck is a visual representation of the most compelling facts about your business. It's a story that needs to be told quickly, so keep each slide short and include pictures and other graphics.

In most cases, you'll be presenting your deck and briefly discussing each slide in a way that adds value to what your audience is seeing. However, in some cases investors will want to preview the deck, so you'll want to make sure it stands on its own.

While every business is unique, including the following slides in your deck should help spark interest from your audience:

- Your business description in a nutshell (about 150–200 words).
- Your target market, including ideal customers and how you intend to reach them.
- The entire competitive landscape, which includes more than just your direct competitors.
- The problem you'll be solving and who you'll be solving it for.
- Your product or service and how it solves the problem.
- Marketing strategy, including your understanding of how your target market buys, your sales process, and which sales channels you'll use.
- How money will flow into the business, including a description of revenue streams, pricing model, and who will be paying you.
- Validation of your idea, including any milestones your business has already met, proof that your solution works to solve the key problem, and a map of your upcoming goals.
- Your core team and the experience and expertise they're bringing to the company.

Your pitch deck could include additional slides depending on the type of business and business stage. For example, a company that's been in business for six months could have a great deal of sales data and customer experience to include. Remember though, here less is more. Keep it short and don't add information simply to make your deck look more impressive.

Show, Don't Tell

Storytelling will draw in your audience more than a simple recitation of information. For instance, giving examples of the problems your potential customers deal with rather than stating the problem will resonate more than statistics and facts, especially when they're problems that your audience can relate to.

COMMON PITCH MISTAKES

When you're new to pitching, it can be hard to get everything right, particularly when you're pitching to venture capitalists and other potential investors. These people see an ocean of pitch decks every year, and they're looking for businesses that truly stand out. Perfecting your pitch deck gets you one step closer to funding. So, as you're putting your presentation together, take care to avoid these common mistakes:

1. Using too many words—think bullet points, not paragraphs.
2. Including more than ten to twelve slides.
3. Sending your pitch deck as a PowerPoint instead of as a PDF.
4. Presenting your pitch deck as a PDF instead of as PowerPoint slides.
5. Not creating a story that flows.
6. Including overly optimistic financial projections.
7. Missing typos, grammatical errors, or design mistakes.
8. Sending the deck to investors who don't invest in your business type, vertical, or stage.

Running your deck by other people can help you avoid sending out an imperfect pitch. You'll only get one chance with an investor, so you want to make a striking impression rather than striking out.

What's a Vertical?

In business terms, a vertical refers to a specific target market or niche that serves a narrow group of customers. This allows a company to focus directly on a particular area so they can gain a competitive edge, targeted expertise, and concentrated customer communication.

GET HELP IF YOU NEED IT

Not everyone is great at selling themselves, writing compelling copy, and designing an eye-catching pitch deck. If you're struggling to create your pitch deck, hire someone to help. Getting this right can mean the difference between generous funding and running out of cash. In addition, it takes a lot of time and creative energy to build an effective pitch deck, which will limit how much you can focus on your actual business.

Depending on the size and scope of your pitch deck, you can expect to spend between $3,000 and $10,000 to have someone create it for you. Make sure you feel comfortable with the person you hire to create your deck. You want this to reflect you and your company, not just a one-size-fits-all package they have prepared. It's worth it to talk to a few creators before making your choice and not just going with the cheapest option. You can use a variety of professional pitch deck creators, such as Deck-Works (www.deckworks.co) and Donna Griffit (www.donnagriffit.com). If your budget is tight, you can also find deck creators and consultants on online platforms like *Upwork* (www.upwork.com).

KNOW HOW MUCH MONEY YOU'LL NEED

Count Up the Cash

Preparation is key for a successful start-up. And one of the first things you'll need to pull together for your business is your start-up costs. Expenses start immediately, before your business fully launches and long before revenues start rolling in. You'll need to cover those costs somehow, but you can't do that if you don't have a realistic sense of how much money you'll need.

Many people vastly underestimate how much it will cost to start and run their businesses, focusing more on the sales side of the equation. But for most new small businesses, money flowing out will exceed money flowing in for at least the first few months. If you don't have a proactive plan for those expenses before you start racking them up, your business could run out of money before it even has a chance to take off.

UNDERSTANDING WHY STARTING COSTS MATTER

A lot of new entrepreneurs jump straight into the deep end without having any idea of how deep the water actually is. They see stories on social media or hear about a friend of a friend who had a great business idea and the money just poured in. While these overnight success stories do happen, they're rare. You will want to know how much starting a business costs before you get started.

Once you compile a list of your probable start-up costs, you'll be able to use that information in several important ways. You will be able to calculate your runway, shore up your business plan, figure out your break-even point, reasonably estimate profit potential, plan taxes for your business, attract investors, and get loans.

Equally important, you'll have an honest sense of when you might be able to start pulling money out of your business, rather than pouring it in.

Finally, investors and lenders know how much money it takes to get started. If you ask for less than they think you need, your application may be denied.

LIST YOUR START-UP EXPENSES

No matter what kind of business you're starting, you'll have some common start-up expenses. After those, you'll have some that are particular to the type of business, such as whether you're selling products or services and whether you'll have a brick-and-mortar location or an online-only presence.

Start-up expenses that many businesses will have include:

- Business formation and registration costs
- Phone and Internet
- Utilities
- Computer and printer
- Software and apps
- Website creation and maintenance

- Security (physical and web-based)
- Office space
- Office furniture
- Insurance
- Market research
- Marketing and marketing materials (brochures, business cards, etc.)
- Professional fees (such as lawyer, accountant, and virtual assistant)
- Supplies
- Business permits and licenses
- Payroll (including yourself)

If you'll be selling some kind of physical product, you'll also need to include inventory and related costs, such as warehousing and shipping. If your business will have employees, you'll need to account for salaries, payroll taxes, workers' compensation insurance, unemployment insurance, and employee benefits. If you'll be buying or renting space, you'll need to include all of the additional costs associated with your potential location. If you decide to incorporate your business or create an LLC, go to the website for the secretary of state or state business office for your company's home state to learn what types of costs you'll face.

DON'T FORGET THAT YOU NEED TO GET PAID

Many new entrepreneurs forget a crucial expense when crafting their start-up budgets: paying themselves. If you've gone all in to build a business and have no other reliable source of regular income, you need to account for your salary here. In this case, then figure out the minimum amount of money you need to cover your personal monthly expenses. You can do this by listing your essential expenses, the ones you need to survive: housing, food, medicine, transportation, childcare. While you're in start-up mode, you may need to cut back on nonnecessities. But including your total monthly essential expenses as your minimum viable salary in your business expenses will make sure you can cover them.

ADD NUMBERS TO YOUR EXPENSE LIST

Now that you've identified which start-up expenses your business will likely incur, it's time to estimate the costs. Some will be easy to figure out because they're fixed and readily available, such as monthly Internet, software subscriptions, business permits, and rent. Others will be harder to pin down. It's difficult to estimate things like employee costs, professional fees, marketing campaigns, and insurance before you actually have those things in place.

Do your best to find realistic costs for each expense through online searches and calls to potential service providers. Look online for average salaries using sites like *Payscale* (www.payscale.com), *Indeed* (www.indeed.com), and *Glassdoor* (www.glassdoor.com). If you have a mentor or connections working in similar businesses, ask them to help you come up with reasonable numbers. You can also tap into resources like SCORE to get help figuring all of this out.

Know the SCORE

SCORE is a network of volunteer business mentors who can help guide you through the start-up process. In addition to a mentor matchup service, SCORE also offers a Startup Roadmap course and tons of free DIY resources for budding entrepreneurs. You can find out more about SCORE, including how to find a mentor, on their website at www.score.org.

DEVELOPING A FINANCIAL SNAPSHOT

Now that you know how much each expense will cost, you'll want to put it all together to create a high-level financial snapshot. This process starts with dividing your expenses into three main categories: one-time, monthly, and recurring but not monthly.

One-time costs include computer equipment, incorporation fees, logo design, and website creation. Monthly costs include payroll, rent, utilities, website maintenance, and advertising. Recurring costs include renewable business licenses or permits, insurance, and legal fees.

Now that you've sorted your expenses into these time-based categories, you can project out the monthly and recurring costs for 1–5 years (many banks and investors want to see five-year projections). Add up all three types of costs to figure out how much money you'll need to get started. It will also help you get a sense of your runway, the amount of time you have before your current cash supply runs out. For example, if your business expenses will be $3,000 and you have $12,000 available, that's four months of runway.

WORKING WITH INCUBATORS OR ACCELERATORS

Programs That Give You a Head Start

Many people think incubators and accelerators are the same—they're not. While both help foster new small businesses, they go about it in different ways, primarily based on the stage of your start-up. Incubators offer a variety of resources for very early-stage start-ups and shepherd them through to growth stages. Accelerators help companies who have already turned their idea into a saleable product and help them build their sales more quickly.

Both of these collaborative programs can help a small business achieve success. They offer guidance, tools, and resources that most new entrepreneurs can't access on their own. If you can take advantage of an incubator or accelerator to get your business off the ground, it's well worth it.

INCUBATORS

Just like their literal counterparts, business incubators nurture start-ups from their early days, even when they're still in the idea phase. Incubators tend to serve several small businesses at once, fostering a sense of community and connection, which can help new entrepreneurs avoid the isolation that often comes with starting a business. Advantages of working with an incubator include:

- Office space or coworking space outside your home office
- Collaborative atmosphere

- Conference rooms
- A physical business address you can use instead of your home address or a post office box
- Workshops
- Access to support services, such as bookkeeping
- On-site mentors
- Interaction with industry experts

Incubators tend to focus locally to encourage regional economic development. They are backed by public funds, though they may also accept private grants. Many incubators are set up as nonprofit organizations.

While there are no strict start and end points for the companies that utilize incubator services, many companies move locations after hitting major milestones. Graduates frequently return as mentors of their former incubator to help other new companies.

ACCELERATORS

Accelerators are geared toward start-ups that have outgrown the idea stage but haven't yet hit their growth spurt. To be selected for participation, your start-up usually will need to have at least a minimum viable product, or MVP. Once in the program, there will be hard and fast entry and exit dates, and sessions usually last between 3–6 months.

Accelerators are normally industry specific and focus more on growth than development. They provide disciplined programs designed to promote your product and connect you with funding opportunities, accelerating your company's growth faster than you could do on your own. Many accelerators work directly with angel investors and venture capitalists (VCs) to help the small businesses in their program succeed. You'll learn more about these investor types later in the book.

Accelerators typically provide capital to the companies they enroll, and in exchange, they receive a piece of the business. Different accelerators require different stakes, but the range is generally 7%–10% of the company equity. Well-known accelerators include:

- Y Combinator (www.ycombinator.com)
- Techstars (www.techstars.com)
- 500 Global (https://500.co)
- MassChallenge (www.masschallenge.org)
- SOSV (www.sosv.com)

Applying to an Accelerator

Accelerator programs accept 10% or less of the companies that apply, so it's important that you apply to the right program and that your application stands out. Most accelerator programs have specific criteria that applicants need to meet, which may include start-up stage, primary location, and industry. Once you've found a good fit, you'll begin the process, starting with your application. An application will tend to ask a lot of questions about your product or service, current traction, your team, and other factors important for success. While you want to answer their questions, you'll want to leave some room for conversation and follow-up questions. Make sure that all must-have information is easy to access with links to presentation materials, references, and financial data.

Once your initial application has made the cut, your business will move along to the next stage in the process: assessment. That's when the accelerator team will evaluate your business for its potential and the viability of what you plan to sell. If your application makes it through the assessment phase, you'll be invited for an interview in which you'll have about 20–30 minutes to show your passion for your team, your product, and how much progress your business has made. At this stage, you'll also provide more details, including things like full financial statements, legal documents, and other information to back up any claims you've made about your company.

The next step can be the hardest: waiting to hear whether your business will receive funding and a place in the accelerator program. Typically, about half of the companies that make it through the interview phase will get a spot in the program.

Your MVP

In business lingo, an MVP refers to a basic starter product that has great features to attract paying customers, particularly early adopters. This is not a prototype but rather a working, usable product to sell and collect customer feedback. Once you receive comments and criticism, you can fix problems and add more benefits to the product based on customer experience.

WHICH IS RIGHT FOR YOUR BUSINESS?

The main way to figure out whether to choose an incubator or an accelerator is by looking honestly at what stage your start-up is in. If your small business is still in the idea phase or doesn't yet have an MVP, start with an incubator. They offer more hand-holding and can help you focus and develop your business idea, whereas an accelerator expects a higher level of knowledge and experience.

If you're looking for a long-term collective where you can bounce ideas off of other entrepreneurs, an incubator will serve you well. If you're itching to get your product out the door and secure the funding needed to ramp up production, you may be better off applying to an accelerator program.

Accelerators can be more competitive about their application process. If your business doesn't quite make the cut, you can work with an incubator to help you get ready for an accelerator. Some incubators feed directly into accelerators, so if that is your eventual goal, you can seek out an incubator program that offers this option.

CHOOSING THE BEST BUSINESS STRUCTURE

From the Ground Up

If you've been on social media, you've probably heard a lot about limited liability companies (LLCs)—and most of what you've heard is wrong. While LLCs can be a good structure for many businesses, it may not be right for yours. So, before you dive in and form one, take a minute to consider your other options.

Every business has a legal structure that determines, among other things, how the company will be run and how it will be taxed. Your business will fall into one of the following business structures: sole proprietorship, partnership, C corporation, S corporation, and LLC.

SOLE PROPRIETORSHIP

If you work for yourself with no business partners, you're automatically a sole proprietor unless you take steps to incorporate your business. Most freelancers and people with side gigs are sole proprietors. It's the most common business structure for small businesses, especially those without any employees.

With this business form, there's no separation between the business and the business owner for legal or tax purposes. Business income shows up on your personal tax return by way of IRS Schedule C. And legally speaking, business liabilities are personal liabilities and vice versa.

PARTNERSHIP

When two or more people own an unincorporated business together, it's automatically considered a partnership. Each partner is a general partner, completely liable for all business debts and able to enter into contracts on behalf of the business.

Partnership agreements lay out the details and structure of the partnership. This includes information such as: each partner's roles and responsibilities, how profits will be split for tax purposes, and how and when distributions will be made.

Though there's no legal requirement to have a partnership agreement—and most small partnerships don't bother with them—it's a good idea to have one. If you don't and legal issues arise, the state's boilerplate version will rule.

Like a sole proprietorship, partnerships don't pay their own taxes, though they do file informational, federal, and state tax returns. The business income flows through to the partners' personal returns in whatever proportion they've agreed upon.

Limited Partnerships

Limited partnerships have at least one general partner and one limited partner. The general partner takes on the responsibility of the business, running the day-to-day tasks and making the decisions. Limited partners, sometimes called silent partners, provide funding but don't participate in the business in any other way, and they are also legally protected against personal liability for business debts.

C CORPORATION

A C corporation, or regular corporation, is a distinct entity—its own "person." The corporation pays its own taxes and deals with its own legal issues. Owners are called shareholders or stockholders, and their percent of ownership in the business depends on how many shares of stock they own.

Maintaining a corporation takes time, money, and effort. There are specific legal requirements that must be followed to retain corporate status, such as choosing a board of directors and holding regular board meetings. Corporations must be registered in the state they're formed, the state where they maintain primary headquarters, and often in any states that they regularly do business.

Corporation owners can get paid in one of two ways. If they work for the company, they'll receive a regular paycheck. Shareholders and shareholder-employees can also receive dividends, a portion of the business profits. This is where corporate double taxation comes into play: the corporation pays taxes on its profits, and the shareholders pay personal income tax on the portion of profits they receive as dividends.

S CORPORATION

S corporations are pass-through entities, meaning the business doesn't pay its own income taxes and the profits "pass through" to the tax returns of the owners. Like C corporations, S corporation owners are called shareholders, and their percent of ownership depends on the number of shares they hold. However, there are several restrictions on S corporations, including:

- They must be domestic (not foreign) corporations.
- They can't have more than one hundred shareholders.
- All shareholders must be US citizens or residents.

S corporation shareholders who work for the company must be paid a regular salary. All shareholders may receive distributions, a portion of profits. Shareholders will be taxed on their proportional share of profits (based on the percent of shares they own) whether or not they receive distributions.

LLC

An LLC is purely a legal construct designed to provide liability protection to small business owners. Its owners are called members, and there can be any number of members in an LLC.

LLCs don't exist for income tax purposes. An LLC will be taxed based on the underlying business form. For example, a single-member LLC will be taxed as a sole proprietorship. A multimember LLC will be taxed as a partnership. And LLCs that elect to be taxed as corporations will file corporate tax returns.

DEALING WITH LOGISTICS

Once you've selected a business structure, it's time to deal with the specific start-up logistics. The first thing you'll need is a Federal Employer Identification Number, usually called an FEIN or EIN. Don't let the name confuse you: Your business will need an EIN whether or not it has employees. The EIN is like a Social Security number for your business, and you'll use it for a lot of things, from opening a business bank account to filing your business tax return. With straight sole proprietorships and partnerships, you can apply for your EIN at any time. With LLCs and corporations, you can apply for the EIN after the business entity is officially formed. You can apply online on the IRS website (www.irs.gov) and get your EIN immediately.

If your business will have a "fictitious name" or a DBA (doing business as), meaning it won't be operating under your name, or the public-facing name won't match the one on your LLC or corporation formation documents, you'll need to register that name. Depending on where your business was formed, you may need to file that with the state's secretary of state or at the county level. Before registering the name, make sure it's not already taken by searching the state database for the name you want to use. This will only tell you if a name is in use, though, and not whether the name has been trademarked. To avoid problems down the road, do a thorough search for the name before you start using it.

Some chores you may also need to do are: Get a state seller's permit, register for a sales tax ID, register for a state employer ID, and get any business-specific licenses or permits (like a liquor license). Though these chores are not the exciting portion of business ownership, they are necessary. Ensure you don't leave anything to the last minute!

HOW SELF-FUNDING WORKS

Me, Myself, and I

Many new entrepreneurs dig into savings, including retirement accounts, to launch their companies. This strategy comes with some benefits, but it unfortunately comes with more drawbacks. That said, it's one of the most common ways to fund a start-up because it doesn't require much work.

If you're starting a cash-light business that doesn't need a lot of resources to get going, self-funding can be a good option. This works well for service businesses, especially when your start-up is a side gig and you have a solid source of current income. It's usually not the best option for companies that require a lot of cash to get started, such as inventory-heavy businesses, or businesses that require costly machinery and equipment.

Before you dip into your savings, though, figure out a rough budget for the first few months of your business. You'll want to know how much runway you have before the business becomes self-supporting, or you'll need to find additional funding.

What's Runway?

In start-up lingo, *runway* refers to how many months your business can operate before it runs out of money. This is based on its "burn rate," or how much cash it burns through monthly. For example, if your business has $5,000 of expenses every month and $15,000 in the bank, it has three months of runway.

WHERE THE MONEY COMES FROM

When you're funding your own venture, all of the money going into your business comes from you. Whether that's a slice of your other income (if you have another job, for example), savings, retirement funds, or personal credit cards, self-funding your business will eat up your personal resources.

Before you start pulling money, figure out how much you have available to put into the business. This calculation is basically an inventory of your cash and near-cash resources. This could include things like:

- Personal checking
- Personal savings
- Emergency savings
- Nonretirement investment accounts
- Savings bonds
- Retirement accounts
- Salary
- Investment income
- Other incoming cash flow (such as royalties)
- Credit cards (personal)

If you're thinking about starting and self-funding a business, consider stashing as much as you can into savings and boosting your credit score before you take that plunge. The more resources you have available, the easier it will be to allow your business the time it takes to start bringing in cash.

THE BENEFITS OF USING YOUR OWN MONEY

The main benefit of bootstrapping—funding your business yourself—is control. You have complete control over every facet of running the company, from marketing to pricing to which bookkeeping software to use. While you may get input from other stakeholders, the ultimate decision-making power is yours. You also won't have the pressure of trying to please investors or lenders, or the issues that come with opposing opinions when you're dependent on someone else for funding.

Another plus: You don't have to spend time and energy trying to impress investors and lenders. You can pour all of your focus into building the business, which can get you up and running more quickly. You'll also be able to pivot and react faster when challenges and opportunities arise.

You'll also learn how to be creative when it comes to business budgeting. Being forced to seek out low-cost or free options for some expenses will help you save money while still keeping your business running. Your creative and problem-solving mindset can come in handy even when cash starts flowing in, as you're able to run lean and maximize profitability.

USING PERSONAL CREDIT CARDS AND LOANS

Though it sounds like borrowing, using personal credit cards and taking out personal loans or home equity loans actually counts as self-funding. This is because you are personally responsible for paying this money back, so it's still coming out of your resources. If you have very good credit and are confident in your ability to meet monthly payment obligations, this can be a quick way to feed more cash into the business.

But it does come with potentially significant drawbacks. If you're unable to pay credit card balances in full every month, you'll rack up interest charges. And even though you're using this money to fund your business, it's still personal debt, so the interest will not count as a business expense. The same goes for personal loans and home equity loans, which have an interest component built in.

If you do have difficulty making monthly payments in full and on time, it will affect your personal credit score. That can lead to higher interest rates and lower credit limits, both of which will limit your ability to borrow in the future. So, you will only want to lean on these resources if you're confident your business will pay you enough to cover the monthly charges.

THE DRAWBACKS OF SELF-FUNDING

Self-funding your business comes with several drawbacks to consider. The biggest drawback: You're limited in how much money you can supply to the business. If you need additional funding, you'll have to start from scratch to find it. By the time you run low on money, it may be harder to convince lenders or investors to provide funding. And if you run out of cash, your business will crash.

Another big drawback: tax consequences. If you pull money out of retirement accounts, make sure you remember to factor in the tax hit. Not only will you have to pay income tax on your withdrawals (unless you're properly pulling contributions from a Roth IRA), but you may also have to pay an additional 10% IRS penalty if you're under age fifty-nine and a half. So, if your business needs $10,000, you'd have to pull approximately $13,000 to $17,000 from your retirement account to cover state and federal income taxes depending on your personal tax situation.

Then there's the debt. If you've used credit cards and loans to fund your business, you have to pay them off even if the business isn't bringing in enough money. Should your business fail, you'll still be responsible for all of this debt, which could take years—even decades—to pay off. You also run the risk of needing to declare personal bankruptcy if you're unable to pay back these debts. The risk factors for self-funding are huge, so only go this route if your business plan accounts for any financial setbacks.

HOW TO BORROW MONEY

Get By with a Little Help

A business loan can help get your fledgling company off the ground, covering your most pressing start-up costs. While it can be hard for start-ups to meet the requirements for a regular bank loan, that's not the only option. Many online lenders will provide loans for new businesses. Plus, businesses that may not qualify for loans may qualify for company credit cards. And you can always turn to the SBA, the US Small Business Administration, where the primary goal is to support small businesses.

Borrowing money for your business works differently than taking out a personal loan. If your company doesn't have its own credit history—and possibly even if it does—the lender will look at your credit score as well, and you may be expected to personally guarantee the loan. You'll also want to make sure you're applying for the right kind of financing for your business because there are a few options out there, such as online loans, SBA loans, business lines of credit (LOC), business credit cards, and asset-based financing.

Each of these options comes with benefits and drawbacks, so it's important to understand all of the loan terms and the potential risks of the loan. Loan terms include the interest rate, payment schedule, length of the loan (such as three or ten years), and prepayment or late payment penalties.

HOW SBA LOANS WORK

Many lenders consider start-ups and small businesses to be high-risk borrowers. That's not surprising when you consider the alarming business failure rate, but it does make it harder for small companies to get funding. That's where the SBA comes into the picture.

The SBA offers several loan programs for small businesses but doesn't actually lend the money itself. Rather, it guarantees the loan for whatever participating lender, usually a bank, actually supplies it. These loans typically come with lower interest rates and more flexible terms compared to loans not backed by the SBA.

DIFFERENT TYPES OF SBA LOANS

When considering an SBA-backed loan, you'll have several options to choose from. Each loan program has its own lending cap and specifies how the loan proceeds can be used. Depending on which loan you apply for, the timeline from application to funding can take anywhere from 1–3 months. These loans typically require a personal guarantee from anyone who owns at least 20% of the company. Here's a quick look at the most popular SBA loan programs:

- 7(a) loans: Loans of up to $5 million that can be used to cover business expansion, machinery purchases, and working capital.
- Microloans: Loans of up to $50,000 that are offered by community-based lenders for start-ups and growing businesses.
- Community Advantage loans: Loans of up to $350,000 that are offered to young start-ups (no more than three years old) in underserved communities otherwise unable to obtain other financing.
- 504 loans: Loans of up to $5 million that must be used for major business purchases, such as real estate or machinery, and the business must come up with 10%–20% of the loan amount.

Watch Out for Predatory Lenders

The online lending world is full of predators, but you can avoid them if you're careful. Predatory lenders often charge extremely high interest rates, include hidden collateral clauses in contracts, and make it nearly impossible to pay off their loans on time. Never sign an agreement that has blank spaces or makes you uncomfortable in any way.

LOAN LINGO

The world of borrowing money comes with its own language. Here are some important terms you need to know so you can fully understand your loan agreement:

- APR (annual percentage rate): The complete yearly cost of borrowing money, which includes the interest plus any fees associated with the loan.
- Default: When the borrower does not pay back the loan as outlined in the loan agreement, usually meaning three or more payments in a row have been missed.
- Amortization: A formula applied to fixed-rate loans to determine the portion of interest and principal to be applied for each loan payment.
- Late fee: An additional cost charged by the lender when loan payments are overdue.
- Origination fee: Loan-related expenses that the lender deducts from the loan proceeds, usually to cover things such as processing and administration costs.
- Loan term: The specific period of time over which the loan must be repaid.

All you need to know about your loan will be spelled out in the loan agreement. If there's anything you don't understand, ask about it before you sign.

ASSET-BASED FINANCING

When your business owns assets, they can be used as collateral for a loan, a product called asset-based financing. It works sort of like a car loan: You borrow money to buy the car, the car serves as collateral for the loan, and if you don't pay, they take your car away. The difference here is that your business already owns the assets and is borrowing money for other reasons, like working capital. Assets that can be used for this type of financing include machinery, equipment, real estate, vehicles, accounts receivable, and inventory.

When your business has collateral, the loan becomes less risky for the lender. That can result in better loan terms for your business, such as lower interest rates. The downside: If you miss payments, the lender can seize your assets.

What Are Accounts Receivable?

When your business sells to customers on credit, where they can buy now and pay later, that's known as accounts receivable in accounting terms. That money will be coming to you eventually when customers pay their bills, you just don't have access to the cash yet.

GETTING A BUSINESS CREDIT CARD

One of the resources to get for your company is a business credit card. You may have to apply based on your personal credit and guarantee the card, but it's well worth doing that. As long as you use it wisely, a business credit card can deliver several benefits for your company:

- Access to extra funds when you need them
- Easy expense tracking
- Credit building in the company name
- Rewards points (if you get a rewards card)
- Quick way to pay vendors
- Cash flow management

The key is to use the card when you can afford to pay the charges, just like with a personal credit card. Whenever possible, try to take advantage of introductory offers that include no or low interest on the card to minimize the interest that will increase business expenditures.

ATTRACTING INVESTORS

Be a Money Magnet

Equity financing often makes sense for small businesses that require more start-up capital than they could reasonably borrow. In these arrangements, investors provide funding in exchange for an ownership stake in the business. But with millions of entrepreneurs after the same limited pool of investment funds, you'll need to show that you can deliver a big return on their investment in order to secure the best chance to obtain funding for your business.

YOUR STRUCTURE MAY LIMIT INVESTMENT

Investors typically demand an ownership stake in the companies they invest in. That means the legal structure of your company will need to be able to accommodate new investors, and not all business structures are designed to do that. Right off the bat, sole proprietorships and general partnerships can't usually accommodate investors. S corporations have strict limits on who can be a shareholder. So, as you're creating your company, consider whether you'll want to allow for outside investors before you settle on a business structure.

The best business structures for taking on investors include C corporations and limited partnerships. In both of these, additional owners may have differing ownership percentages, and both offer limited liability—meaning they can't lose more than their investment—to the investors. C corporations are more popular options because they allow for the business to go public in the future.

Going Public

Most small businesses start out as privately owned companies with a limited number of owners. When a company "goes public" or has an IPO (initial public offering), anyone can begin to buy shares of the company over a stock exchange. Once the flip switches, the company transitions from privately owned to publicly owned.

WHAT INVESTORS WANT

Investors want to make money on their investments, just like you do when you invest in something. But since your new small business hasn't yet proven itself, it's more of a gamble for the investor. So they will want to see compelling evidence that your company will offer big returns in the near future. To that end, investors need to be convinced that your business will be a moneymaker, and that will take some work on your part.

First, you'll need a professional, comprehensive business plan. Investors want to know that you're serious about success. Make sure the plan includes all the basics, such as target market analysis, marketing goals and plans, timelines and financial projections, and strategies to deal with future challenges. The plan should highlight what's unique about your product or service and why it's better than anything already out there.

Next, you'll need to show them solid performance numbers. If you've already been in business for a little while, you'll have those available. If not, you'll need to create realistic projections that you're able to back up with research. Some of the specific performance data investors look for include:

- Gross margin (gross profit): The difference between your total sales and the cost of goods sold, which shows how much profit the business generates before overhead expenses.
- Net income (or net loss): Also called the bottom line, this shows what the business has left after all expenses have been paid, which may be negative (a loss) for new businesses.
- Revenue growth: Current sales compared to sales from a prior period, usually last month or last year, shown as a percentage calculated as [(current sales minus prior sales) divided by prior sales].
- Monthly recurring revenue (MRR): The amount the business brings in every month, demonstrating stable monthly cash flow.
- Customer acquisition cost: How much it costs the business to get a new customer, which is typically more expensive than retaining an existing customer.
- Churn rate (attrition rate): The rate at which your company loses customers over a set time period, which is especially important for subscription-based businesses.
- Liquidity: How much cash the company has, which shows investors whether the company will be able to cover expenses during the coming year.

Investors know that start-ups may not have great numbers in every category but expect that to be balanced out by other important metrics. Don't be tempted to mess with your numbers—you'll be expected to prove them, even estimates. But do highlight the positives as much as you can.

ANGEL INVESTORS

Angel investors, or private investors, tend to be people with extremely high net worth who want to back small business start-ups that they believe in. In exchange for providing funds, they take an ownership stake in the company. Their funding can come in a single lump or as ongoing financial support as funds are needed.

Many angel investors take on a key role in managing the business day-to-day. That gives you an in-house mentor to help move your business forward, which can help your company succeed more quickly than without their guidance. It also means, though, that you won't be in sole control of your business and how it's run. With that in mind, you'll want to make sure that you and your angel make a good team. Ultimately, even if the money is good, you may not want to accept money from someone you can't imagine working with every day. You can start your angel search on websites like *Angel Investment Network* (www.angelinvestmentnetwork.us) and *Angel Capital Association* (www.angelcapitalassociation.org) or at networking events targeted toward angel investors.

Beginnings on Broadway

Back in 1978, a professor at the University of New Hampshire coined the phrase "angel investor" describing wealthy individuals who provided financing for Broadway theater productions. Once the shows started generating ticket sales, the angel would be paid back from the proceeds.

VENTURE CAPITALISTS (VCS)

Venture capital (VC) firms specialize in equity financing, typically taking at least 20% of the ownership shares of the companies they invest in. With that, they often require some level of management control, which will be spelled out in the deal agreement. After all, VCs are in it for the money, expecting substantial returns on their investments.

These firms usually only look at larger start-ups with fast growth potential, often in the tech sector. VCs tend to put their money—often $2 million–$5 million—into businesses on track to go public in the future. They make big bets in the hopes that they'll hit the jackpot with the next big thing. Not surprisingly, there's fierce competition for VC funding, and only a small percentage of applicants walk away with contracts.

VCs take their time vetting the companies they're considering, so don't expect a quick decision here. They know they're making a risky move by investing in an unproven start-up, so they do what they can to minimize the risk. Each VC has its own criteria for evaluating and accepting businesses. To attract their attention, your business will need to show: a solid business concept, an innovative product with a significant competitive advantage, a business plan, strong metrics, an experienced management team, and a heavily researched, sizable target market.

Bottom line: If you want to attract VC funding, come prepared. Remember, these investors are looking to get in and out quickly, moving your business to a stage where it's likely to either go public or to be bought out by another company. If that's not what you want for the life of your business, look for other funding options.

ACCESSING GRANTS AND OTHER FREE START-UP MONEY

Yours for the Taking

Free money aimed at start-ups can jump-start your small business without you needing to take on debt or give away control. This financial assistance mainly comes in the form of grants, but you may be eligible for prizes and special tax credits. Unlike loans, this money doesn't have to be paid back, making it a preferred source of funding for many start-ups.

However, there is a possible minor downside: Many grants and prizes result in tax liabilities, as they may be classified as income. Check with an accountant about whether any free money your business receives will be taxable. That way you can plan ahead and reserve some cash to pay the eventual tax bill.

SMALL BUSINESS GRANTS

There are hundreds of grants available to small business owners, provided by government agencies, private companies, and non-profits. These grants are typically financial awards given to small businesses to help them cover essential expenses while they're in the start-up and growth phases. Unlike loans, grants rarely need to be paid back—they're free money for your company. In some cases, the money must be used for specific things, like hiring employees or implementing green initiatives. In other cases, the money can be used for anything not included in restrictions, like bonuses for owners or paying down existing debt. Make sure to fully understand the terms of the grant before you start spending.

BE PREPARED

Grant applications (also called grant proposals) can take weeks to complete, especially if you don't have basic information about your business ready to go. Plus, application windows can be quite short, sometimes just a few weeks from posting to deadline. You'll want to have as many building blocks prepared as possible so you can quickly jump on these opportunities as they arise. Though each application could have some unique requirements, there are some items that many want to look at, such as:

- Grant request summary/executive summary
- Up-to-date financial statements
- Mission statement
- Company website
- Company social media profiles and posts
- Need statement
- Project budget and action plan

Create these components as soon as you can, so when you need them, you can simply tweak them to match the particular requirements of the grant you're seeking.

UNDERSTAND GRANT PARAMETERS
BEFORE APPLYING

Just because grants deliver free money doesn't mean there are no strings attached. In many cases, there are restrictions on how you can spend the money. For example, a local revitalization grant may be limited to beautifying a storefront or getting new signs. Some grants require matching funds, meaning you have to put a set amount of money into the project as well. Most government grants require regular financial reporting and may request additional data related to the grant. They will verify that your company is spending the grant money according to the grant parameters. If it's not, your company will almost certainly have to return the funds and could potentially face legal issues (such as fraud charges).

If a grant doesn't align with your current business goals, it's not the right grant for your company. For example, if you want to invest in new technology, a neighborhood revitalization grant is not a good fit. Don't spend your time and energy applying for grants that don't make sense for your business plans.

The Office of Women's Business Ownership (OWBO)

The OWBO helps women start and grow businesses through their partnership with the SBA. They provide services such as training and counseling, along with access to federal contracts and funding. Their goal: to "level the playing field" for women entrepreneurs. You can find more information about the OWBO and their Women's Business Centers on the SBA website at www.sba.gov.

BEWARE GRANT SCAMS

Sad but true: There are a lot of scammers pretending to offer grants or facilitate the grant process. Some will ask you to pay them in exchange for shopping your grant proposal around and submitting it on your behalf. Others are phony grants that require a steep application fee. How can you avoid these scammers? Be wary of anyone asking you for money. And rather than just doing Google searches for "small business grants," rely on these trusted resources:

- Grants.gov
- SBIR.gov (Small Business Innovation Research)
- SBDC on SBA.gov (Small Business Development Centers)
- NASE.org (National Association for the Self-Employed)
- MBDA.gov (Minority Business Development Agency)
- DBE on Transportation.gov (Disadvantaged Business Enterprise)

Many state and local governments and nonprofit organizations have dedicated small business grant programs as well. Just remember to verify that they're legit before you start the process.

CROWDFUNDING

Crowdfunding is a relatively new way to raise money for your startup, using a form of social media to attract attention from numerous small investors. Crowdfunding platforms are websites that work sort of like other social media sites but focus on letting users raise money from their followers. Unlike VCs and angel investors, crowdfunding supporters don't get a piece of the company in exchange for their money. And unlike lenders, crowdfunders don't expect to get paid back with interest. Rather, they usually get some other form of reward, such as free products and early access.

CONTESTS

Small businesses with great stories behind them can enter contests for cash prizes. These contests aren't as common as grants, but they can come with substantial winnings. Typically, these contests are open to small businesses with fewer than one hundred employees and revenues under $5 million (but requirements will vary).

To enter, you'll have to provide minimal information about your business for eligibility requirements and write a compelling essay about your business: how it's helping your community, allowing you to follow your passion, or supporting your personal growth after you faced and overcame a challenge. Prizes can run from $2,500 to $60,000.

Some of these small business contests include:

- America's Top Small Business Awards (US Chamber of Commerce)
- Barclays Small Business Big Wins Contest
- FedEx Small Business Grant Contest (a sort of combination between a grant and contest)

You may also find small business contests run by local corporations or universities. The parameters for these prizes are usually less restrictive than those of grants, inviting even fiercer competition.

Chapter 3

What Will You Sell?

Your main product or service will be the basis of your business, but how do you know it's the right choice for your business? Do you have the up-front cash to fund an ample product supply? How many service hours can you actually work every week? These questions and others will help you decide what kind of product or service feels right for you.

Once you figure out if your business will be product- or service-based, you'll build from there. That decision will drive most other aspects of your business, including how much you need to sell to cover costs, when you'll be able to pay yourself, and how big your team will need to be. Your decision will also determine how much growth potential your company has and how easily you'll be able to scale up if customer demand increases.

When you create products, you have to protect them. So whether you've got a warehouse, a garage, or a closet full of inventory, you need to build a system to manage and track it. There are so many factors that come into play, especially for product sellers, and it's important to have everything in place so you can be ready when that first sale comes in.

SELLING A PRODUCT VERSUS PROVIDING A SERVICE

What You Have to Offer

If you're in business, you're selling something. That something is either a product or a service, and in some cases, it can be a little of both. Products may be physical or virtual, and the customer owns them once they're purchased. Services are actions that you do for a customer, where they get the benefit of what you've done but don't own anything additional afterward. Hybrids—a mix of product and service—give customers a little bit of both, like an auto repair that includes any needed parts for purchase and the labor to install them.

What you sell dictates a lot about how you'll run your business. It affects start-up capital needs, pricing, overhead expenses, physical space needs, profit margins, and much more. Once you figure out what you want to sell, many of your business decisions will flow from there.

TYPES OF SERVICES

There are two main categories of services: business to business and business to consumer. Companies that provide services to businesses support other companies' infrastructure, profitability, and growth. Companies that provide services directly to consumers fill some kind of need that the customer can't (or would rather not) manage on their own.

Examples of business services include:

- Social media marketing
- Cybersecurity
- Tech support
- Legal
- Copywriting
- Accounting and tax
- Graphic design

Examples of personal services include:

- Massage
- House cleaning
- Handyman
- Tax planning and preparation
- Medical
- Financial advisory
- Tutoring

When you sell a service, you're really selling yourself and your employees. Success depends on your skills and expertise as well as your customer relationships. Start-up and ongoing costs are generally lower than product-based businesses because your main products are time and effort, rather than an inventory that requires physical space. That's why these types of businesses are easier to start and fund and generally deliver higher profit margins.

PROS AND CONS OF SELLING SERVICES

In many ways, service businesses are easier to start than businesses that sell products. However, service businesses also face some drawbacks that product-selling businesses do not encounter. Keep the plusses and minuses of each in mind before you settle on one type of business. Benefits of selling services include:

- Less cash outlay: Savings on physical space, product-related purchases, safety testing, and quality control.
- More manageable cash flow: No need to buy and pay for items before you sell them, causing a negative cash flow imbalance during start-up.
- Easy pivoting: You can quickly take advantage of new technologies and adjust to changing market conditions.
- Customize for client needs: You can design or modify service packages based on individual client specifications.
- Client relationships: Generating long-term relationships with customers reduces turnover and increases profitability.

On the downside, when selling a service, it can be more difficult to describe what you do to prospective clients and how your services provide value. Potential clients may be hesitant to buy from you or take longer to court, as they can't really test-drive a service like they could with a product. In their eyes, it's hard to know what may separate your service from a competing business.

TYPES OF PRODUCTS

There are two main types of products: physical and digital. Physical products can be further subdivided into durable, nondurable, and perishable goods. Durable goods last at least three years, rarely need to be replaced, and tend to come with big price tags. Examples include dishwashers, lawn mowers, and chairs. Nondurable goods—such as clothes, makeup, bottles of wine—need frequent replacement, either because they get used up or don't last long. Perishable goods are really a subset of nondurable goods. They include products that have a very short shelf life, and the quality of the product declines quickly. Examples include fresh flowers, fruits and vegetables, and dairy products.

With physical products, your business may sell at any point on the chain. For example, you could sell raw materials or ingredients to manufacturers, create products to sell using raw materials, or buy and resell finished goods.

Virtual Goods

Unlike digital goods, virtual goods have no place in the offline world. They exist and are bought and sold in online communities and games. If you've ever made an in-app purchase or bought a new skin for your character in a video game, you've bought virtual goods.

Digital products are bits of media that can come in many forms, such as courses, ebooks, apps, photos, online games, and songs. Once created, they can be sold repeatedly without any additional cash or creative outlay needed. They come in a wide variety of formats, including PDFs, MP3s, streaming services, printables, and plug-ins.

PROS AND CONS OF SELLING PRODUCTS

Like anything, selling products comes with pros and cons. The biggest pro: You're selling something easily identifiable and uniform over and over to many customers. This offers some consistency for planning and cash flow purposes. It also makes marketing simpler, as customers have the opportunity to check out the product before they buy it.

On the downside, selling products—particularly physical products—calls for a bigger cash investment both up front and ongoing. Product sales come with smaller margins, though volume can help minimize that effect on the bottom line. It can also be tricky to properly estimate how much inventory your business needs to have on hand to meet demand without overstocking and tying up valuable resources (like space and cash). Finally, products—including digital products—are subject to theft, loss, and damage.

KNOW HOW MUCH YOU NEED TO EARN

Make a List, Check It Twice

You want your business to be self-sustaining and for it to provide income for you. So, you need to know how much it will cost to run the business. At first, you likely won't foresee every possible expense, but including everything you can think of on your plan will help you figure out how much your business needs to earn to sustain you financially and make profits.

Your eventual earnings will be a product of your pricing, how many customers you have, and how often they buy from you. You can project different possible scenarios to see how a variety of situations will affect the amount of money your sales bring in. These projections will show you when your business may be profitable.

COMMON BUSINESS EXPENSES

There are some expenses that are common to most businesses. That's true whether you're renting office space or working from home, or whether you're selling a product or providing a service. Any cost your company incurs that is necessary and ordinary (in IRS language) counts as a business expense. Typical small business expenses include phone(s), utilities, software and apps, marketing and advertising, legal and professional fees, office expenses, bank charges, insurance, and taxes and licenses.

Product-based businesses will also have expenses related to inventory, such as packing materials, shipping, and storage. Your start-up may have additional expenses not included in this list.

COVERING YOUR PERSONAL EXPENSES

When you've gone all in on building a small business, meaning it will be your primary source of personal income, you'll need to factor in your living expenses to figure out how much your business needs to bring in. This calculation can get overlooked when developing business budgets, but it's a crucial part of the equation.

When creating a personal budget, you'll want to create a staggered budget that separates essential living expenses, necessary expenses, and wants. Essential living expenses include only the basics that you'll need to survive, like food, rent/mortgage, utilities, medication, transportation, and childcare. Necessary expenses include things you need but can survive without, such as annual checkups and nonurgent medical care, homeowner's insurance, and routine car maintenance. Wants include things you could live without but don't want to, like streaming services or dining out.

For the purpose of your business budget, your minimum paycheck has to be able to cover your essential living expenses. If you do have some other sources of reliable income, you can deduct that amount from the amount your business income will need to cover. Once your company is posting steady profits and positive cash flow, you'll be able to pull out more money for your personal expenses.

DON'T FORGET TAXES

Whether your business pays its own income taxes or passes its income to you for tax purposes, taxes are one of the biggest expenses business owners face. They are also one of the biggest expenses that new small business owners fail to account for as they're figuring out how much revenue they need to bring in. A general rule of thumb is to set aside at least 35% of income for taxes. That may sound high, but it includes both federal and state income taxes, self-employment taxes, and employers' payroll-related taxes.

When you own your own business, you'll likely have to deal with quarterly estimated income tax payments. That means paying out big lump sums four times a year rather than small amounts weekly like you do with a regular paycheck. Accounting for those payments ahead of time will help you avoid the extra expenses of IRS penalties and interest. If you have employees on payroll (which may include you if your business is set up as a corporation), you'll also have to regularly remit (send money for) payroll taxes.

PLANNING FOR PROFITS

You're in business to make money, and that means you need your business to be profitable. This means that money coming in from sales needs to exceed money going out for expenses. Once you have a realistic sense of your business's expected expenses, you can start to figure out how much you'll need to sell to end up with a profit.

By playing around with business components, you'll be able to calculate roughly how much inventory you need to move or how many service hours you need to provide.

BUILDING BLOCKS OF A BUDGET

Your business needs a budget: a plan for how expenses will get paid. The budget will be a flexible, living document that changes as you learn more about how cash flows through your company and as your company grows. A written budget gives you a point of comparison. You'll be able to see where you've over- or underestimated expenses, notice when your business is doing better (or worse) than expected, and make better business decisions. It will also serve as a key planning tool for the future, letting you know when you'll be able to hire employees, buy expensive new equipment, or expand your business. Your budget will also provide early warning signs for inadequate cash flow and let you know if you're spending more money than you have.

Knowing how much money you need to run your company is half of the budget equation. The other half is knowing how much money is available to cover expenses and where that cash comes from. A standard budget starts with revenue, but that may not work if your start-up hasn't yet generated any sales. For now, your revenue section can include loans or investor funds allocated month by month. Once you're ready to launch and start bringing in revenue, you can use a conservative estimate for your budget as a benchmark.

Business Budget Templates

Never put together a business budget before? Start with a template. You can find many free sample budgets on websites such as www.sba.gov. Your accounting software may also provide budget reporting, or you can create a budget in a spreadsheet software from their templates.

FINDING YOUR BREAK-EVEN POINT

Your Business's Balancing Act

When your company breaks even, it means your revenues exactly equal your expenses, so there's no profit or loss. The break-even point is where that happens, the precise spot where the revenues can cover all of the expenses. Once you know what that break-even point is, you can make better business decisions and run your business more effectively.

Figuring this out is just the first step. It can take months or years for a small business to finally reach its break-even point and stop running at a loss. Having a sense of when a business stops losing money can make it easier to attract investors, get loans, and manage your business.

HOW THE BREAK-EVEN POINT CAN HELP

Calculating the break-even point for your company before you launch helps ensure success. The break-even point tells you the minimum dollar amount of sales required to produce profits and can potentially show other issues that will impact your bottom line. Working out this calculation can help you figure out:

- Optimal pricing and different price points.
- Reasonable sales goals.
- Overlooked expenses.
- Whether this business can be profitable.
- Whether it makes sense to launch a new product or service.
- How well and quickly the business can recover from setbacks.

The break-even point is also a crucial part of your business plan, letting potential investors and lenders know that your business has profit potential.

BREAK-EVEN LANGUAGE

Break-even is an accounting term, and you must use accounting terms and equations to figure out how to calculate it. The lingo can get a little confusing if you haven't taken courses in cost accounting. So, here's the basic vocabulary you'll need to move forward:

- Fixed costs: Expenses that stay the same no matter how much you sell, like rent, salaries, and insurance.
- Variable costs: Expenses that change based on production or sales, such as packing and shipping materials, or production supplies, like glue or screws.
- Semi-variable costs: Expenses that have both a fixed and a variable component, such as electricity or repairs and maintenance.
- Contribution margin: The difference between the unit sales price and variable unit cost of what you're selling divided by the unit sales price [(unit sales price minus unit variable cost) divided by unit sales price], which lets you know how much each unit helps cover overhead costs.
- Unit: One of what you're selling; for example, rocking chairs or service hours, where one chair or one hour would be a unit.

Now that you've got the lingo down, you're ready to start calculations.

HOW TO CALCULATE THE
BREAK-EVEN POINT

Determining the break-even point requires a bit of accounting math. You can figure it out by using either dollars or units. In order to calculate the break-even point, you'll need to have total fixed costs, unit sales price, variable unit cost, and sales projections in units.

Now comes the math. The basic formulas look like this:

Break-even point (units) equals fixed costs divided by (unit sales price minus variable unit cost).

Break-even point (dollars) equals fixed costs divided by contribution margin.

Let's look at an example. Suppose your business will be selling picture frames. The fixed costs add up to $5,000 per month. The variable costs that go into each picture frame come to $1, and you sell the frames for $10 each. In order to break even, your company would need to sell 556 frames per month: $5,000 / ($10 - $1). Alternately, in dollars, the business would need to generate $5,556 in frames sales to break even: $5,000 / ([$10 - $1] / $10).

Pad Your Predictions

Calculating the break-even point for a start-up relies mainly on estimates, as you'll have no historical sales and expense data to pull from. Most new entrepreneurs tend to underestimate expenses because they can't foresee every cost that will come up. So, it makes sense to add an extra 10%–12% to your expected costs to cover any unexpected expenses.

PRICE, COST, AND VOLUME CHANGES

The factors that go into calculating your break-even point won't stay static over time. On top of that, you may want to change them proactively to see what kind of effect it would have on your company's profitability. This experimentation can be helpful when your business is struggling, such as during a recession or if there are other issues that drive sales down. If sales decrease, you may not be able to hit the break-even point, which could make it impossible to pay all of your vendors and suppliers. When you face an unexpected decline in sales, you can use the break-even formula to see the effects of different options, such as raising prices or cutting costs.

One option: reducing variable costs by negotiating with suppliers or finding new ones. If you can bring the variable costs down from $1 to seventy-five cents, for example, the break-even point would drop down to 540 frames.

Perhaps you can reduce fixed costs by taking a temporary salary cut—for example, bringing the fixed costs down from $5,000 a month to $4,500 a month. By doing that, your break-even point would drop down to five hundred frames.

Price, costs, and sales volume are all closely connected. The decisions you make about any of these factors will affect your break-even point and your business. So, using the formula to proactively see the expected effects of different choices can help you make better decisions for your company.

USING THE BREAK-EVEN POINT

Once you've run a break-even analysis—a set of the different outcomes created by using different assumptions—you'll be armed with information. For example, in order to break even, your company will need to sell at least five hundred picture frames every month to be viable. Your next step is deciding whether that outcome is realistic.

If selling that quantity seems like a breeze, you could have a successful business on your hands. If it seems possible but difficult, look for other areas to cut expenses so you can achieve a more manageable sales volume goal, or find the funding to carry you through the initial lean period until you can establish a stronger sales volume. If you think it's nearly impossible to hit that volume, then this may not be a viable business idea.

Another important thing to remember: You cannot predict or control customer demand. If you can't generate enough interest in your product or service, or if consumer demand for it simply drops off or disappears, your business may not ever be able to break even.

SETTING YOUR PRICING

The Price Is Right

Coming up with a pricing plan for your products and services involves striking a balance between what they're worth and what customers will pay. This can be especially tricky for new business owners to figure out. Many start-ups will tend to undercharge in an attempt to ramp up sales, a strategy that can quickly put them out of business.

FACTORS THAT GO INTO PRICING

As you begin to create your pricing policies, you'll need to look at several factors. Many of these are math-based, which you or a business partner can easily calculate. Others involve the emotional impact on potential customers, which can be a little trickier to navigate, especially when you're just starting out. You will want to keep the following factors in mind:

- Your sales goals
- Market demand
- Purchase or production costs
- Overhead
- Competitor pricing
- Desired profit margin
- Customers' disposable income
- Consumer psychology and price perception

You may not get the pricing just right at first, but you can adjust as you learn more about your customers.

What Is Overhead?

In business terms, overhead refers to the ongoing costs of running your company that are not directly related to the products or services you sell. Examples of overhead expenses include rent, utilities, accounting fees, office supplies, and marketing costs.

VALUE-BASED PRICING

Value-based pricing involves setting prices based on the perceived value of what you're selling. This customer-focused strategy works best for services or high-quality products (like artwork) that can be personalized or offer the buyer a unique experience. This system relies heavily on what differentiates your product or service from others and understanding what your customers will buy if they don't buy from you.

The extra value of what you're selling must be made clear to customers. One key driving factor is scarcity or exclusivity: There's only one original copy of this painting, or there are only three slots available for you to take on new coaching clients. You must also have a deep understanding of your target market and what drives their buying decisions.

COST-PLUS PRICING

Also known as markup pricing, cost-plus pricing is exactly what it sounds like: You start with the cost of whatever you're selling and add a fixed percentage to that to come up with your price. Here's how it works: Suppose you're selling sweaters in your online shop. Each sweater costs $30 to make and ship, and the associated overhead costs are $10, making the total cost $40 per sweater. You want a 20% profit, so you add that to the cost to get to your price of $48 per sweater: $40 (cost) × 1.20 (markup) = $48 (price).

Cost-plus pricing is an easy to way to price your products, but it leaves the customer out of the equation completely. This can work well for mass-produced products or as a starting point for other pricing methods.

COMPETITIVE PRICING

This pricing strategy works well for businesses that sell common products sold by many other companies. There are three options for this strategy: setting the same price as your competitors, pricing higher, or pricing lower. Which will work best for your company depends on things like your sales goals, special services offered, and available upsell products.

Premium pricing, or pricing higher than the competition, can work when your company creates a more welcoming environment for customers. This environment may include special payment terms, add-on features, or a higher-quality experience that attracts customers to your company even though your prices are higher than a competitor's.

Underpricing your competitors can draw in customers, but unless you have additional products to sell or upsell, you could end up taking heavy losses. This "get them in the door" strategy can work well to attract new customers, where you'll have the opportunity to turn them into long-term loyal customers.

OFFERING DISCOUNTS

A good rule of thumb when it comes to discounts: Offer them when it benefits you. You can use special one-time discounts to attract new customers. You can offer discounts to customers who prepay or pay early. You can offer referral discounts to customers who bring you new customers or for repeat business (like punch cards). In all of these cases, your business reaps the benefit of the discount either through new business or improved cash flow.

However, many small business owners—especially service providers—feel obligated to offer discounts without an upside for their company. They may feel like their prices are too high, or that no one will choose their services without an additional incentive. This could mean that your marketing is targeting the wrong group of potential clients or that your pricing doesn't align with what you're providing. Most likely, you're offering discounts because you're feeling insecure about what you're providing.

WHEN AND HOW TO RAISE PRICES

Increasing your prices can feel scary. You may be afraid that you'll lose customers, and you might, but that doesn't mean you shouldn't charge what your goods or services are truly worth. For new business owners, it can be tricky to tell when you should raise your prices. Here are a few guidelines to help you decide:

- You have plenty of customers, but you're not breaking even.
- Your prices are substantially lower than your competitors.
- You're charging for your services by time rather than by value.

Once you've decided to change your prices, you'll need to communicate with your customers. Your best bet is to inform them ahead of time and let them know why, especially if you emphasize any added value for them. Stress that the increase will ensure continued or improved quality, but don't overexplain and don't apologize. Some customers will complain, and some will leave. In fact, if no one complains or leaves, your prices are probably still too low.

If you're concerned about losing too many customers, especially in service businesses, you can increase prices for new customers only at first. Let your existing customers know about your new pricing and how long they can continue to enjoy their current pricing. For example: "As of March 1, we will be increasing our prices. Because you've been a valued loyal customer, your price will not increase until June 1."

You can also use an upcoming price increase as a way to drive immediate sales. When you give your customers advanced notice of the increase, you can also give them the opportunity to buy more now or lock in current pricing by prepaying for services.

MAKING SURE YOUR BUSINESS IS SCALABLE

Prepping Your Business for a Growth Spurt

Businesses grow more quickly now than ever before. With easy access to large pools of potential customers and new markets, your business has almost unlimited growth potential—as long as it's scalable, that is. Scalability refers to your company's ability to quickly adapt to increasing demand and heavier workloads. That means increasing work capacity and ramping up productivity without disproportionately increasing costs. In fact, you'll really want to scale and decrease costs simultaneously to boost profitability. All that depends on the scalability of your business and overcoming common limitations to growth.

THE BIGGEST ANTI-SCALABILITY TRAP

New small business owners often fall into a trap that hampers their ability to scale their businesses: They do everything themselves. Why? They're good at what they do and can complete tasks quickly and correctly every time. They don't want to waste cash on tasks they could do, like bookkeeping and marketing, even if it's not their specialty. They focus on profitability *now* without an eye to the future.

When the business depends 100% on you to get everything done, growth is limited by your time and capacity. You're working *for* your business instead of working *on* your business. This is particularly true in service-based businesses, such as consultancies, where the main product is also you and your skills. Your business simply can't grow past the amount of time you can give it without making some significant changes.

Scale Yourself

You may be the whole business, but you can allocate pieces of what you do to others easily! You can hire people to do things like transcribe your presentations into blog posts and social media posts, combine blog posts into sellable booklets, and use AI and apps to cover things like scheduling and email summaries.

HOW TO SET UP YOUR BUSINESS FOR EASY SCALING

You want your business to grow the right way, including increased customer base, sales, and profitability. In order to hit this success trifecta, you need to set up your business now for quick and easy scaling later. Take these steps to set up a scalable foundation:

- **Find the funding to enable scaling.** Bootstrapping can only take you so far, so figure out how much money it will cost to make your business scalable. You may need additional staff, more space, or new tech to take your business to the next level, and that all costs money. Look into grants, loans, or investors to fund your growth plans.
- **Add the right people to your team.** When you surround yourself with competent, trustworthy people, you can focus on being the best entrepreneur you can be. Find professionals with integrity, experience, and specialized skills so you can work on building your business.

- **Delegate as much as you can, whenever you can.** Delegating only when you're too busy to do something keeps your team from stepping up. It can be anxiety provoking at first to hand off tasks, but practicing this critical skill is crucial if you want to scale.
- **Embrace technology.** By carefully investing in the right tech, your team will be able to work more efficiently. You'll be able to automate some tasks, minimizing busywork and freeing up time for you and your team.
- **Document whatever you can, from systems to processes to troubleshooting.** Every time you develop a system or a process, make a mistake and fix it, or figure out a better way to do something, document it. You want your team to have detailed instructions and a clear idea of how to do their jobs.
- **Create processes that can be scaled.** As your business scales up, you want the average unit cost of work to drop. Finding ways to make it easier and faster to do repetitive tasks will increase efficiency, which will result in better margins as you grow.
- **Foster a collaborative environment.** Good ideas can come from anyone, and you want your team to feel comfortable voicing their thoughts. Hosting brainstorm sessions and open meetings make everyone feel involved and valued. A team that feels listened to and appreciated will keep coming up with innovative suggestions, helping your business in unexpected ways.

SCALE YOUR SALES

You can set up your business for scalability, but you still need to bring in the customers and make the sales to achieve real growth. The purpose of scaling is to increase sales, and this requires planning. A plan starts with a look at your sales system, from lead generation (attracting new potential customers) to collections (getting payments from customers). Some factors to consider are: lead magnets (special deals or free resources given to potential customers in exchange for contact info), sales funnels (the journey customers take from learning about you to purchasing), lead tracking (evaluating where potential customers are in the sales funnels in order to keep them engaged), and follow-up customer onboarding, ordering systems, customer service, invoicing systems, and account management.

Making sure all of these processes and systems work smoothly will help your business generate and fulfill increasing sales without missing a beat. And while bringing in new customers and closing more sales drives growth, you want to make sure your billing and collections process is solid. Sales without payment won't help you scale—it will make your business fail.

WHEN IS THE RIGHT TIME TO SCALE?

When your business is ready to scale, you'll see clear signs. Scaling is a big undertaking that often costs money and time, so it can't be done on a whim. It can't be done, at least not successfully, because you need more sales to keep your business viable. Scaling requires having the right technology and personnel in place so you can seamlessly meet increased demand without having to scramble. So, how do you know when it is the right time? Here are a few signs:

- Your business has positive cash flow and cash reserves.
- Your business has been steadily profitable for at least six months.
- You have loyal repeat customers.
- Your business is meeting or beating set goals.
- You've had to turn away customers due to limited capacity (inventory, people, or time).
- Your current systems can be easily expanded to handle more leads, sales, collections, and customer support.
- You have the technology in place to automate basic tasks.
- You have a well-trained staff who are ready to take on more responsibilities.

If your company is showing at least a few of these signs, it could be the right time to scale. Take a hard look at the business to make sure it's ready because premature scaling can lead to business failure. Among the most important factors is the company cash position because scaling will (at least temporarily) drain cash and potentially reduce positive cash flow.

PROTECTING YOUR INTELLECTUAL PROPERTY

That's My Idea!

Intellectual property (IP) includes anything you dreamed up in your mind: website content and design, information products, inventions, logos, trademarks, and more. These are intangible assets, meaning they don't have physical form, but that doesn't mean they don't have value. As our society and economy become more information based—think social media—there's a lot more IP floating around. This wealth of IP can lead to misuse and theft unless you take the proper steps to protect it.

A lot of things fall under the IP umbrella, but for business purposes there are five main categories: digital assets, trademarks, patents, copyrights, and trade secrets.

Each type of IP involves different kinds of assets and different forms of legal protection. And while your primary focus will be protecting your own IP, you'll also want to make sure you're not accidentally infringing on someone else's.

DIGITAL ASSETS

If your business has a website, online content, digital products, or a proprietary algorithm, it has digital assets. These can be vulnerable to unauthorized use and hackers—think about our society's issues with rampant illegal downloads or copied content. This illegal activity makes it critical to properly protect your digital assets as valuable intellectual property. To secure these assets, you'll want to take the following critical steps:

- Establish ownership and value of all digital assets (write an inventory list).
- Limit access with passwords, secure links, encryption, and watermarking.
- Copyright or trademark whenever possible.
- Create and implement a strong cybersecurity plan.
- Back up your property to a secured external hard drive or server.

Taking all of these steps will help protect your digital assets. You may also want to consider getting a specialized insurance policy to protect against loss or theft.

TRADEMARKS

Your brand identity will play a big part in your success as a small business owner, and that's why it's so important to protect it with a trademark. Anything that helps consumers recognize your company and distinguish it from others falls under that trademark umbrella. A few examples are slogans, logos, company names, phrases, symbols, designs, and sounds.

All of these creative components make your brand unique. But that doesn't mean other people won't swipe your logo or slogan to use for their business—without your permission—to cash in on your success. A trademark offers solid protection against this and gives you standing to sue anyone who copies your branding.

Before you register your trademark, do a thorough search to make sure no one else is already using it. While you can DIY the trademark process on the US Patent and Trademark Office website, it's a good idea to work with a trademark attorney to make sure everything gets covered and filed properly.

PATENTS

Patents are exclusive property rights for an invention granted to the inventor by a government agency (such as the US Patent and Trademark Office). The invention can be a physical product, like a light bulb; a design, like an app; an improvement or add-on feature; or a process, like a streaming service platform. Most patents are utility patents that last twenty years from the date of issuance and require maintenance fees periodically. Design patents, which in this sense refer to appearance only, last for fifteen years from the grant date and include things like specific emojis and fonts.

COPYRIGHTS

Like the name suggests, copyrights give people who create original material the exclusive right to use or copy that material (think authors and songwriters). With a copyright, the creator can authorize others to use that work with a licensing agreement. Copyright protection lasts for the life of the creator plus seventy years. Unlike other forms of protection, copyrights happen automatically when work is created, but you can take extra steps to make sure others don't copy your work without permission. You can register the work through the

US Copyright Office, which includes filing an application and paying a fee. This makes it easier to sue anyone who uses your creation. You may also protect your work (though not as thoroughly) by:

- Including the © symbol on your work.
- Sending the work to yourself via email or snail mail.
- Using Creative Commons (www.creativecommons.org) to get a free copyright license that allows you to share the work with others in any way you choose.

You may be wondering what kind of creations can be copyrighted. Along with books, poems, and plays, you can also copyright website content, research, computer software, and works of art.

Who Owns It?

If your company hires freelancers or contractors for creative work, make sure the contract clearly states that those works will belong to the business, and it will hold the copyright. This can help you avoid sticky situations and possible lawsuits brought by the creator.

TRADE SECRETS

If your company has developed a process, technique, or recipe that's valuable and kept closely guarded, you have a trade secret. This confidential information gives your business a competitive edge and must be protected. One way to protect your secret is to have anyone involved in creating, using, or working with it sign a nondisclosure agreement, or NDA. If any signers disclose even a part of that trade secret, they're in violation of the agreement and can be penalized. Other steps you can take to protect your trade secret include:

- Physical security: Restricted areas, trackable employee ID badges, video surveillance, log entry system for access, proper disposal of sensitive information.
- Cybersecurity: Computer event logs to track files accessed, periodic password changes, multi-factor authentication for remote access, updated antivirus and antimalware software, employee trainings on suspicious emails and websites.
- Insider threat awareness: Disgruntled employees, excessive or undisclosed foreign travel, repeat security violations, unexplained wealth.

Trade secret theft is on the rise and often involves recruiting employees by temptation or coercion. Cyberattacks are frighteningly commonplace in today's world. So, taking these crucial steps to secure your trade secret will help protect one of your company's most valuable assets.

MANAGING PHYSICAL PRODUCT INVENTORY

Keep It Moving!

Selling physical products calls for more math and logistical data than selling services. You'll need to balance your available space, customer demand, supplier timelines and pricing, company cash flow, and more to figure out the optimal amount of inventory to keep on hand. Inventory management is one of the toughest things for new small business owners to get right. You can lose business when you don't have enough product on hand, or you can lose money when you have too much in stock. Finding the sweet spot takes time and experience, but eventually you'll get close enough for your business to succeed.

HOW MUCH INVENTORY DO YOU NEED?

Balancing cash flow, customer demand, and inventory levels is hard. Too much inventory and you run the risk of tying up too much money and resources for little or no returns, especially if your inventory can go bad or become quickly outdated. Too little inventory and you run the risk of losing customers to the competition or needing to pay higher "get it fast" prices to your suppliers. With time and experience, your inventory instincts will improve.

You'll need to consider storage space, product shelf life, seasonal merchandise, inventory costs, and how long it takes to restock before you determine your inventory levels.

Once your business has some sales experience to draw from, you'll be able to see how quickly your inventory moves. Seeing patterns in your inventory will allow you to make better purchase decisions and increase profitability.

COSTS ASSOCIATED WITH INVENTORY

Selling physical products comes with more costs than you might expect, especially if you're manufacturing or creating products for sale. But even when you're simply reselling finished products, inventory-related costs add up and reduce your profit margins. Typical costs associated with inventory include direct product costs (including delivery fees to your location), storage space, stocking (putting products on shelves), displays, insurance, labor, spoilage or shrinkage, and interest (if you're borrowing money to buy inventory).

Inventory-related expenses are also called "carrying costs." These add up quickly and require extensive cash outlays before any sales money can start coming in.

UNDERSTANDING COST OF GOODS SOLD

Cost of goods sold (COGS) is an accounting term used to distinguish the expense of the products you're selling from the other business expenses. Any cost that goes into producing, purchasing, or preparing the products you're selling eventually makes its way into your COGS.

A lot of new business owners get confused about their COGS and how it relates to inventory. The products you have on hand make up your inventory. Products that you have sold go into your COGS. Sounds simple enough, but it can get awkward accounting-wise, especially if you don't track your inventory piece by piece and need to figure it out at year-end.

The basic equation to calculate your COGS looks like this:

([Beginning inventory plus purchases] minus ending inventory) equals COGS.

Let's say you're selling books. At the beginning of the year, you have $100 worth of books in inventory. Throughout the year, you buy $500 worth of books. So the total number of books available for sale during the year came to $600. At the end of the year, you have $50 worth of books left in inventory. That means your COGS for the year was $550: $100 + $500 - $50 = $550.

In your profit and loss calculation, COGS gets deducted directly from your total sales number to come up with the gross profit, also sometimes called the "margin." The margin refers to how much money is left in your sales to cover the regular operating expenses—bigger margins mean bigger profits.

INVENTORY MANAGEMENT SOFTWARE

If you're going to maintain inventory, you'll need to track it. While you can do that manually or in spreadsheets, a better choice is to use dedicated inventory management software. Effective inventory software covers a lot of necessary ground and should help you:

- Track inventory in real time.
- Scan barcodes or enter new inventory.
- Organize your warehouse storage.

- Connect to your POS system.
- Forecast demand based on sales experience.
- Avoid shortages with low-inventory notifications.
- Pull flexible inventory reporting.
- Analyze inventory trends.
- Reduce inventory carrying costs.
- Take inventory counts and perform audits.

While there are some good general inventory management applications, such as Katana and Lightspeed, dedicated industry software can be more useful. For example, booksellers might use Basil or Anthology, which are specifically designed to manage books and related inventory. Restaurant owners might use a program like Lightspeed Restaurant or TouchBistro. Look at the options for your industry before you choose your inventory management software.

Can't My Bookkeeping Software Do It?

Some bookkeeping programs, like QuickBooks, come with a general inventory component. While these are better than nothing, they don't offer as much flexibility, accuracy, or support as industry-specific inventory tracking software. The best option: inventory management software that integrates with your bookkeeping software for all-around accurate reporting.

DROP-SHIPPING

If you own an online business that sells products, drop-shipping may be the easiest way to manage inventory. Drop-shipping uses an order fulfillment center to deliver products to your customers, where your company essentially acts as a middleman connecting customers and products. This frees up resources that your company would have had to invest in inventory, so you don't have to come up with as much cash to start your business. It's also easier and faster to start with drop-shipping than managing inventory yourself because you don't have to deal with any issues brought on by warehousing, packing and shipping, or tracking inventory. Drop-shipping offers you more flexibility to run your business from anywhere without being tied to a permanent physical location.

Drop-shipping also makes it easier to test different products or product categories you might add to your store. And if your business takes off, you can scale more quickly than if you had to ramp up yourself. The drop-shipper takes on the extra work, the extra inventory, and the extra physical space needed to meet your customers' demands.

On the downside, profit margins tend to be lower. Since it's so easy to start a company that relies on drop-shipping, it attracts a lot of competitors only interested in "lowest price" wars. You also have less control over inventory. For example, you may not know when the drop-shipper is running low on particular products, especially when they're fulfilling customer orders for dozens of companies simultaneously. Customer service issues can crop up when you're working with multiple suppliers that converge in a single customer order. For example, a customer orders five products, and it takes three different suppliers to fulfill the full order. That can result in discrepancies in shipping dates and also cost you more in shipping costs.

MAINTAINING ADEQUATE CASH FLOW

Money In, Money Out

More businesses fail due to cash flow problems than almost any other reason. According to SCORE, about 82% of small business failures can be traced directly to cash flow. Understanding the underlying causes of this pervasive problem can help you avoid premature failure.

Cash flow refers to the way money moves into and out of your business. Money can come in from sales, loans, and investments. Money can move out through paying expenses and taking distributions.

If your business has more money going out than coming in, it's primed for a cash flow crunch. Those can be devastating for small businesses, so it's important to stay on top of your cash position and monitor it carefully and constantly. That's true even if your business is currently doing well financially. It doesn't take much for that condition to change.

COMMON PROBLEMS WITH CASH MANAGEMENT

New businesses crave money. But sometimes when they get that money, they don't carefully plan out how to spend it. Rather than holding on to some working capital, they often make future-based purchases based on their desired growth projections. That can leave them cash poor at a time when their money is key to survival. New small businesses can tie up their cash by:

- Focusing on profits over cash flow.
- Overinvesting in assets.
- Carrying too much inventory.
- Expanding too much or too soon.
- Not maintaining or utilizing credit.

Another common problem for new business owners is not paying enough attention to cash flow. These small business owners are busy wearing a hundred hats, and keeping an eye on the books often gets shoved to the bottom of the to-do list. Neglecting looking at your business's financial status can keep you in the dark about its cash flow and keep you from preventing major problems before they occur.

Count on Your Accountant

No time for bookkeeping, financial reporting, and analysis? Check in with your accountant—they're not only there to do the taxes. A proactive financial professional partner can regularly check in on the business finances and give you advice and guidance on how to prevent cash flow and other financial problems.

PRIORITIZE CASH FLOW OVER PROFITS

When it comes to the survival of your business, cash flow is more important than profits. That concept may seem confusing because most small business advice is geared toward turning profits. But even a profitable business can run out of cash. Sounds wrong, but profits and cash are not the same thing. Profits are the difference between revenue (sales) and expenses. Not all sales result in immediate cash, just like some expenses may not be paid with cash.

If you have profits without sufficient cash to operate, your business won't be able to survive. However, a business with cash on hand has a chance to turn things around and become more profitable, even if it's racking up losses right now.

KEEP CASH RESERVES

Cash reserves for a business work like emergency savings: They're there to help make ends meet when things slow down. Planning for slow times will help you get through them even when they last for months.

If your business has a cash stockpile, whether it's from loans, investors, or past profits, you may be tempted to spend it on new equipment or ramp up marketing to drive growth. Before you do that, figure out how much cash your business will need to go 3–6 months without sufficient revenue, and stash that money into a savings account.

If your business is running smoothly but doesn't have cash reserves, build them now. That may require putting off or slowing down plans for expansion or cutting back on some expense areas. While that may feel uncomfortable right now, you'll be happy for the breathing room if conditions take a turn for the worse.

INVENTORY AND CASH FLOW

If your business has product inventory, it's probably your most expensive asset. Poor inventory management leads to cash flow problems more than any other issue. Here are just some of the ways not keeping tight track of your inventory can drain company cash:

- Not selling items before they expire so they become worthless.
- Ordering items currently in stock because they were misplaced.
- Running out of items due to faulty counts.
- Losing customers because of out-of-stock items.
- Overspending on storage space because of inventory mismanagement.
- Paying higher rush- or small-order prices to fulfill customer demand.

Properly tracking inventory in real time will help you avoid these problems, but more than 40% of small businesses either don't track inventory at all or use notoriously problematic manual inventory systems. Staying on top of your inventory is one of the best ways to minimize cash flow issues.

TAKE ADVANTAGE OF VENDOR CREDIT

If your vendors—the companies your company buys from—offer extended payment terms, use them. Even though you might save money by paying earlier, you'll lose current cash flow, and at the beginning of building a business, cash flow matters more than saving a few dollars. Later, when your business has sustainable positive cash flow, you can take advantage of early payment discounts to improve profitability.

If you haven't been buying on credit, talk with your vendors about how your business can start doing that. It's much easier to get credit when you don't need it and nearly impossible to get it when you do.

UNPAID SALES SLOW CASH FLOW

If your business has a lot of sales on credit, revenues will be high but cash will be low. That can result in crippling cash flow problems unless you take direct steps to improve your customer's timing when it comes to payments. There are a few ways you can encourage your customers to pay on time or even early:

1. Offer prepayment discounts: Having customers pay you in advance can beef up incoming cash. A prepayment discount gives them an incentive to pay now instead of later.
2. Offer early payment discounts: When you invoice customers, you can give them the option of getting a small percentage discount (typically 2%) if they pay within two weeks of the invoice date rather than waiting for the due date.
3. Don't allow credit sales: You don't have to let customers buy on credit; you can insist on payment at the time of the sale. This *might* turn off some potential customers, but when cash flow matters, those aren't the customers you want.

SELLING THROUGH ONLINE PLATFORMS

The Wonders of Modern Marketing

One of the most popular ways to start a business is to open a virtual shop. To do that, your business will need to use an online sales platform. Some of these platforms manage practically every aspect of the customer experience. Others leave the heavy lifting to you and your company website while facilitating the "shopping cart" process. Whether you'll be dropping your online shop into a full-service platform or adding shopping capabilities to your existing website, take the time to figure out which will work best for your business in the long run, including when you're ready to scale up.

Popular platforms include Shopify, WooCommerce, Amazon, and BigCommerce. If your shop will be selling handcrafted items, a platform like Etsy may be the best choice. With so many options available, you'll need to do some due diligence before you choose an online home for your business.

HOW MUCH DOES IT COST TO START A SHOP ONLINE?

Depending on the online retail (also called e-tail) platform and features you choose, the cost to start an online store runs from a few hundred to several thousand dollars. On average, new online shops cost about $3,500 to create. You should expect some (if not all) of the following costs to open an online store:

- Domain name: A unique address for your web shop.
- Hosting: A place to park your website, which may be included with your platform.
- E-commerce software: The program that will let you sell online.
- Theme and design: The appearance of your shop's web pages.
- SSL (Secure Sockets Layer) certificate: A digital verification of your site's identity that allows for an encrypted connection.

Keep in mind, it can be much less expensive to add a shopping cart to your existing website, but the price trade-off may not be worth the added workload if, for example, you'll be selling a wide variety of physical products or don't understand how sales taxes work.

Once you're up and running, you'll have some ongoing costs to cover. That includes things like payment processing fees, annual domain and hosting fees, and data backups. Make sure to budget for both the initial setup costs and the monthly or yearly costs your business will incur to use an e-commerce platform.

The Cheapest Way to Start

Want to launch an online shop with very little money? You can start a bare bones e-commerce site for around $100 and use it to sell digital products that you've created or services your company offers. When customers start buying, you'll face transaction-based costs, which come right out of the sale.

FEATURES TO CONSIDER WHEN CHOOSING YOUR PLATFORM

While pricing may be the main driver of your e-commerce platform choice, there are other things to consider before making a final decision. Base pricing may not include key features that you'll need to get your shop up and running. Make a list of all the features you absolutely need and a second wish list of features you'd like to add when you can. This will help you figure out which platform will be the best fit for your business, even if it's not the least expensive. You'll want to consider these key features when looking for an online shopping platform:

- Whether domain names and web hosting are included.
- 24/7 availability and reliability (after all, if the site is down, your shop is down).
- Integration with the payment choices you want to offer (such as PayPal).
- Scalability. (Will it be able to handle more traffic as your business grows?)
- Reporting and analysis tools.
- Built-in features and integrations.
- Ease of navigating the site and dashboard.
- Inventory management.
- High-quality shipping partners.
- Online learning resources and extensive customer support (for your business).

Considering all of these components in the early stages of your business, even if you don't need them yet, will help your business grow from the start, and you won't need to switch platforms down the road when your business picks up. You'll also want to make sure that the platform you choose can integrate with apps you're already using, like your accounting or CRM software. Think carefully about what you need for your e-tail site, and what would cross an option off the list. For example, if you have a physical store as well as your online shop, can your e-tail platform incorporate that? If not, it's not the right choice for your business.

WHAT ABOUT SELF-HOSTING?

You can set up your own website with online shopping capabilities rather than going with an all-in-one e-commerce platform. That takes some specialized knowledge and skills, which can greatly bump up setup costs, but offers you more flexibility and control over all aspects of your shop. Your company will be responsible for everything from design to security to ongoing maintenance. Unless you (or someone on your team) are an experienced web developer, you'll need to outsource most of these tasks. That will lead to a bigger cash outlay during the setup phase.

You'll still need e-commerce capabilities, like a shopping cart, added on to your website. Site builders like WordPress offer these as plug-ins, but you may need to pay for monthly e-commerce hosting and licensing fees.

A LOOK AT SOME E-COMMERCE PLATFORMS

If you search for e-commerce platforms online, the big names (meaning those that are the most successful or are willing to pay for promoted posts online) are the ones that will dominate your searches. These platforms are well tested and have strong track records, but they're not all right for every business. Here's a quick look inside some of the best online sales platforms:

- **Shopify:** Good for companies that sell physical products and are building their first shop. This platform offers a wide range of apps and integrations, abandoned cart data, and mobile interfaces for customers who shop on their phones. This all-in-one platform offers tools for drop-shipping, payment processing, and marketing.
- **Wix:** Good for very small businesses and solopreneurs who sell services or a limited range of products. Its user-friendly store builder lets anyone create and design their shop. This platform also provides powerful search engine optimization (SEO) tools to help your customers find you easily.
- **BigCommerce:** Good for companies poised for growth. This flexible platform offers guided setup to help you easily build your online store. It comes with dozens of tools and seamlessly supports businesses ready to scale up without missing a beat.

Regardless of the type of e-commerce site or plug-in you end up with, having the ability to sell online will generate more sales to your business. Do not rush into picking one, as some may work better for your business than others, and it can be difficult to make changes after your selection.

Chapter 4

Create Your Dream Team

Starting a business often feels like a solo activity, but it's not. Even the simplest businesses need teams. Your business doesn't necessarily need large teams, or employee-based teams, but your team should have people who will work with you (and for you) as you create a company from the ground up. At first, you may be tempted to just do everything yourself, but you'll quickly learn that it's very difficult (if not impossible) to do so successfully. Too many things will get overlooked, done late or incorrectly, or just plain skipped. The question isn't whether you'll need a team, but who you'll need to fill the gaps and smooth the edges.

Virtually all businesses need some kind of relationship with a lawyer and an accountant because legalities and taxes are two things you do not want to get wrong. If you plan to hire employees, figuring out the ideal team size and creating detailed job descriptions will help you find and bring on the right mix of people. And if you're really not sure what you need, a business mentor or coach can help guide you toward the best decisions.

IDENTIFYING KNOWLEDGE AND EXPERIENCE GAPS

What Don't You Know?

Starting a business requires dozens of skills, like product development, marketing, accounting, managing people, and more. It's impossible for you to expertly perform all of the necessary skills on your own. That can be scary and even make you second-guess your business. After all, if thinking about finances makes you anxious, how will you handle the business budget? Or if promoting yourself feels uncomfortable, how will you market your company? If this business anxiety sounds familiar, you are not alone. Virtually all new entrepreneurs have knowledge gaps. The trick is to fill those gaps the right way.

KNOW YOUR GAPS

You know what you're good at and where your experience shines. But it can be harder to identify the skills you don't have, and you'll want to do that before you launch your business. If you have just a basic understanding or limited experience in an area, or just don't like doing something, count that as a gap for now. For example, if you can't stand working with numbers, list bookkeeping as a gap you'll need to fill. Other common areas that new entrepreneurs often identify as gaps include:

- Taxes (income, payroll, and sales)
- Social media and email marketing

- Content creation
- Human resources
- Cybersecurity
- Tech support
- Website building and management
- Research
- Product development
- Accounting and money management
- Project management
- Team management
- Customer service and support

Identifying your knowledge and skill gaps early on will help you figure out how much help you'll need to start and run your business. Plus, it will give you the opportunity to take the time you need to find the team that can best cover those gaps—whether it's a team of employees, subcontractors, or a combination or both.

Many new business owners try to learn how to do as much as possible by themselves and end up creating problems that need to be cleaned up. Those clean-ups can cost much more than hiring a professional in the first place. While preserving cash may be a priority, think about the big picture rather than individual tasks you think you'll be able to handle with a little training. It's probably not worth your time to learn things that could be more successfully farmed out, like building your website or setting up the company books. Enhancing existing skills and knowledge makes sense; taking on new learning challenges while trying to build a successful business doesn't.

STAY ON TOP OF TECH

Technology changes at an astonishing pace. Software and apps you use today could be obsolete in just a few years. And even if they're still around, the new versions may barely resemble the one you're used to using. With new tech being developed constantly, it's easier than ever to automate routine business tasks, but you have to know how. Keeping pace with new tech can be tough, especially if you're coming from a job where they maintain the status quo. The variety of apps and their uses can feel overwhelming. Even if you're tech savvy, you may not be familiar with all of the tools you can use to start and run your business. Figuring out what tech your company needs will be key to filling technology-related gaps. You can keep up with the latest and greatest by going to trade shows and conferences, networking with other business owners in your industry, watching technology talks, and reading tech blogs and newsletters.

Prioritizing technology will help you run a leaner, more efficient business and enhance scalability. Keeping you and your team current will require constant learning.

Adding AI to the Mix

AI, artificial intelligence, can help get your business off the ground. You can harness the power of AI for marketing campaigns, newsletter writing, research, data analysis, and many other projects. Equally important, you can use AI to help you automate repetitive tasks, an important step in scaling your business.

PRIORITIZE NEEDS

Once you know the areas you'll need help with, prioritize them in terms of importance and timing. For example, creating a website is important and needs to be done ASAP. Accounting, money management, and tax awareness are crucial for keeping your business afloat from day one. Content creation would fall lower in both priority and timing rankings.

Make two columns on a blank sheet of paper. Prioritize each task by importance in column one and by timeline in column two. Any items that have both top priority and urgent timing will need to be addressed first. Your business can't move forward without them, and they need to be handled by an expert. For less important tasks, you have more time to figure out how you'll handle them, including handling them yourself for the time being.

EDUCATION AND TRAINING

If you have the time and capacity, you can learn how to do almost anything. And when you're starting a business and short on cash, it can be more cost effective to teach yourself new skills or enhance skills you have that need polishing. Online courses and tutorials cover virtually every possible skill, making it easier to learn at your own pace while simultaneously beginning to build your business.

Some good options for online training include:

- *Coursera* (www.coursera.org)
- *Harvard Business School Online* (https://online.hbs.edu)
- *LinkedIn Learning* (www.linkedin.com/learning)

- *Skillshare* (www.skillshare.com)
- *SCORE* (www.score.org)

Many software programs come with built-in training modules, robust learning centers, FAQs, and customer support. They may also come with beginner templates and setups to get you started. For example, if you want to learn design skills on the fly, you can start using an app like Canva and learn as you go. Accounting programs like FreshBooks come with predesigned invoice templates, built-in calculators, and tutorials to help you set up your books.

You can also look into certificate programs and courses offered by local universities or community colleges. Many states also offer comprehensive training programs through Small Business Development Centers (SBDC). You can find your local SBDC by searching the listings on the SBA website at www.sba.gov.

If you don't have the time, energy, or desire to learn new skills right now, you can have other people do those tasks for you. However, it makes sense to have at least a basic understanding of everything it takes to run your business, even if you won't be doing the actual tasks yourself. For example, many new business owners count on bookkeepers or accountants to keep track of the numbers, but they should still be able to understand their financial statements and other key metrics in order to run their companies profitably. The more knowledge and skills you gain, the better your chances of building a sustainably successful business.

OUTSOURCING TASKS TO FOCUS ON YOUR BUSINESS

Call In the Experts

Entrepreneurs are "do it" people, often taking on innumerable tasks to start their companies. And when you're also bootstrapping, you hate to spend money on anything you could do yourself. Unfortunately, that's the quick path to burnout and business failure. It makes more sense to spend the money—even if that means you'll have to turn to loans or investors—to get help with tasks. The trick is to get the best quality work done for a reasonable cash outlay, taking tasks off your plate that you can't prioritize yourself. Then you can focus on building your business and claiming tasks that fit in your wheelhouse.

YOU CAN'T DO EVERYTHING

Many new entrepreneurs feel strapped for cash, so they'll try to take everything on themselves. Unfortunately, this can lead to business failure for three key reasons:

1. There's not enough time for you to do everything by yourself, so critical tasks will slip through the cracks.
2. You'll avoid tasks you don't like or aren't good at, constantly shoving them to the bottom of the to-do list where they'll never get done.
3. You'll burn yourself out by overworking—especially if you're working on things you hate doing.

On top of that, with the current pace of technology and change, skills you have now may be obsolete in a few years. New apps and tech stacks (the combination of tools, software, and platforms you use to run your business) can improve efficiency, but you have to know how to use them and integrate them into your processes. Bottom line: Every new business needs a team to make sure all tasks get done properly.

IDENTIFY STRENGTHS AND WEAKNESSES

Before you start looking for help, figure out exactly what your needs are. Using a SWOT (strengths, weaknesses, opportunities, threats) analysis provides you with strategic information to figure out what to do next. A SWOT analysis is usually created as a square with four sections, one for each element of SWOT:

- Strengths: Experience, unique skills, specialized knowledge, or what you're good at.
- Weaknesses: Areas that need improvement, skills you lack, areas requiring more experience, or what you struggle with.
- Opportunities: Technology that can improve your business, goals you're working toward, mentors and network contacts, or how your business can get better.
- Threats: Obstacles to filling skills gaps, strengths your competitors have, or ways your business may flounder.

You can use this method as a starting point to identify any areas that need to be filled in. If you're already working with a partner or a consultant, include them in your SWOT. You don't want to duplicate skills you already have access to, and you don't want to assume someone else has a strength that they don't.

GAIN KNOWLEDGE AND CONNECTIONS

To ready your business for future growth, you'll want to invest in building knowledge bases. That doesn't necessarily mean spending money, but it will mean investing time and focus. There are hundreds, maybe thousands, of online courses and programs in every area you can imagine. Most industries hold events, conferences, and conventions to share the latest tech, gadgets, and information, often with on-site training as part of their marketing.

Business software and apps often come with free trial periods and training programs. You can take advantage of these trials to see which tech solution will work best for your business. Any tasks you can automate with technology will save you time, effort, and money. Many apps come with automation templates that repeat tasks once you set them up. For example, CRM programs can automatically send welcome emails when a new customer joins your list. And tools like Zapier can create automations across different apps that your company is using, such as automatically saving and organizing email attachments to your storage software or automatically posting to Instagram when you publish a blog.

You can also work with consultants to assess your company's training needs and develop custom education programs for you and your team. Acquiring and enhancing the skills you need to move your business forward will be well worth the costs, even if it isn't immediate.

OUTSOURCING

Outsourcing refers to using people outside of your company to do work that could be done in-house. Businesses outsource specific tasks to fill skills gaps and to save money. Though people associate outsourcing with hiring overseas workers, any person or company you hire to take over a piece of your normal operations counts. For example, if you hire another company to handle all of your customer service needs, you've outsourced that task. Commonly outsourced tasks for small businesses include:

- Customer service
- Accounting and bookkeeping
- Cybersecurity
- Administrative tasks
- Payroll
- Human resources
- Manufacturing

Unfortunately, outsourcing has its own drawbacks. For example, you have less control over performance and timing or your company could be at greater risk for security threats. Plus, a string of different contractors may result in inconsistencies in product or service quality. So, if you choose to outsource tasks, make sure you vet whoever you'll be working with and put protections in place to minimize risks. Outsourcing is not the only way to bring aboard help for your business; your team may also be made up of a combination of employees and contract-based workers (also called contractors).

Outsourcing versus Contractors

The main difference between outsourcing and hiring contractors is scope. Outsourcing is the ongoing or permanent use of external resources to manage a portion of the workload that could have been done in-house. Contractors typically work on a temporary basis, and they perform tasks that can't be handled in-house.

WILL YOU HIRE EMPLOYEES OR CONTRACTORS?

The Pros and Cons of Different Workers

Hiring people to take on part of the workload will free up your time to focus on your business's big picture. When you're ready to hire, you'll have two main options: employees and contractors. Employees tend to be more focused on long-term progress and outcomes because they're tied to the company. You set their work schedule, pay, and priorities. Contractors typically work for several companies at a time, on their own schedules and based on their own priorities, which may not match yours. The main reason small businesses hire contractors instead of employees: They cost the company less. But that doesn't mean they're necessarily the better choice for your company.

WHICH IS BETTER?

Both employees and contractors come with benefits and disadvantages. You'll consider multiple factors when deciding the type of team you want to build, and which type of hire would best serve your business. That can change over time and often does. Many small businesses begin with contractors, then grow into hiring employees.

Entrepreneurs often turn to contractors first because they're less expensive than employees, even if their hourly rate is higher. With employees, you—the employer—will be required to pay a variety of taxes, like their Social Security, Medicare, Federal unemployment tax, and state unemployment tax.

In addition, employers usually must maintain workers' compensation insurance if they have at least one employee (the requirement varies by state). Employee benefits may also come into play, especially if you have already established a business retirement plan for yourself (more on those later).

HOW CAN YOU TELL THE DIFFERENCE?

The key factor that determines whether you'll have employees or contractors is control. With employees, you control every part of their work: their hours, pay rate, where they work, and how they work. Your expectations inform how they do their job, and you prioritize what tasks they must do for the efficiency of your company.

When you hire contractors, they have complete independence from your company—it's why they're referred to as independent contractors. They set their own fees, choose when and how you'll pay them, set their own work schedule, and choose where they work. They decide what tools they'll use to complete their projects and whether your company has to reimburse them for expenses. If you are controlling all of those factors, you have an employee even if you're mistakenly paying them as a contractor.

Get a W-9

Before you pay a contractor, have them complete and submit Form W-9. This form is similar to the Form W-4 that employees must complete and contains basic information such as the contractor's name, business name, address, and tax ID. You'll need this information to prepare their 1099s at the end of the year.

USE CONTRACTS WITH YOUR CONTRACTORS

Whether you work with them on a project or monthly basis, make sure that you have a signed contract or engagement letter for every contractor you work with. This benefits your company by clarifying the relationship and specifying the terms of the job. Your contractor agreement should:

- Clearly identify the contractor relationship.
- Spell out parameters for the gig, including job description and deadlines.
- State that the contractor will use their own tools or equipment.
- Provide the contractor's contact information and tax ID.
- Detail invoicing requirements needed for your company to pay the contractor.
- Indicate that your company will own all rights to the work product (especially important for things like content creation or logo design, for example).

Keep your contractor agreements on file along with their completed Form W-9. You will want to have their files in order and easily accessible to keep payments on schedule and to gauge your expectations of their work.

WHEN THE IRS RECLASSIFIES CONTRACTORS

A lot of businesses prefer to hire contractors because they cost less than employees. But just because you call someone a contractor doesn't mean that they fit into that classification legally. If you have control over where, when, and how the "contractor" works and gets paid, the IRS could determine that your contractor is really an employee and reclassify them. For example, if you hire a contractor to answer phones in your offices from 8:00 a.m. to 12:00 p.m. three days a week, they would almost certainly count as an employee in the eyes of the IRS.

If a contractor believes they are actually being treated as an employee, they can file a form reporting the employer's uncollected Social Security and Medicare taxes, which can also lead to reclassification. Reclassifications can cause a lot of problems for your business and cost a lot of money in unpaid employment taxes, back pay, and fines.

The Voluntary Classification Settlement Program

The IRS offers a sort of modified amnesty for employers who voluntarily reclassify contractors as employees using Form 8952. Employers who do this may receive a reduced employment tax bill, minimizing the financial pain of the reclassification. You can find more information on the IRS website at www.irs.gov.

KNOW THE LABOR LAWS

If you decide to hire employees, your company will be subject to numerous federal and state labor laws. These are designed to protect employees, not employers, and violating them can result in big fines. Here's a quick overview of federal labor laws:

- Wage laws: These cover the minimum wage, overtime rules, and equal pay.
- Family and Medical Leave Act: This allows for extended absences from work for eligible employees during illnesses or when caring for a family member with a health issue.
- Discrimination laws: These protect employees from being treated unfairly based on their gender, orientation, race, religion, age, disability, and other things.
- Harassment laws: These deal with hostile work environments, sexual harassment, and other forms of workplace harassment.
- Wrongful termination laws: These protect employees from being fired for illegal reasons such as discrimination or retaliation.
- Occupational Safety and Health Act (OSHA): This protects employees from unsafe work environments like blocked exits or slippery flooring, for example.

You can find out more about federal labor laws at www.usa.gov. As for state laws, you'll have to follow the rules for all states where you have employees working. For example, if your business operates in Maryland but you have remote employees working in Florida, Florida labor laws generally will apply. However, there are exceptions for state laws, as these labor laws can vary widely. You can find out more about state labor laws at the US Department of Labor website at www.dol.gov or on the applicable state's official website.

HOW TO PAY YOUR PEOPLE

Money: It's What They Want

Whether you're working with employees or contractors, they need to get paid. Contractors, like any other vendor, get paid whenever and whatever they bill you. Employees get paid according to your business's wage/salary rate and schedule. Keep in mind that having employees also creates payroll tax obligations that your business will need to meet.

Either way, your business has people to pay. With employees, you'll provide paychecks based on the stated pay schedule, such as weekly, biweekly, or monthly. With contractors, you'll pay based on their invoice terms or the contract agreement. Both types of workers expect to be paid on time, every time. So if you're managing these payments yourself, make sure to pay close attention to the pay schedule. It's easy for new business owners to get overwhelmed and let accounting tasks slip through the cracks. Paying your workers should be top priority, or you'll lose them.

You'll also be responsible for tracking all of the payments and payment details for contractors, employees, and tax authorities throughout the year. With so much to keep track of, you may want to consider using a payroll provider that also manages contractor payments. Yes, it costs money to use a payroll service, but the value they provide will be well worth it.

PAYROLL PROVIDERS

A word of advice: Don't do payroll yourself. There are tons of rules and numbers to remember, and both change seemingly at random.

You have to deal with federal, state, and local tax filings. You have to make tax payments on time, all the time. It's a massive headache and very easy to get wrong.

That's why you'll want to use a payroll provider. They handle everything, from making sure everyone—including tax authorities—gets paid properly, to creating and distributing W-2s at the end of the year, to making sure all filing obligations are met. They keep up with all of the state and federal tax withholding rates, and they make sure your company is always in compliance.

Along with all of that, payroll providers make sure employee withholding taxes and other deductions are calculated properly, automatically figure out overtime pay, and handle wage garnishments. The benefits of outsourcing your payroll far outweigh the drawbacks, mainly that it costs money and you have less control over sensitive employee information.

If you go this route, make sure to use a company with a proven track record for accuracy, timely filings, and good customer service. Just a few of the reliable small business payroll providers include:

- Gusto
- Justworks
- Patriot
- ADP
- OnPay

The right choice for you will come down to pricing, your comfort with the interface, and whether you'll need benefits management along with payroll. Ask other small business owners which provider they use, and ask your accountant if there's a service they recommend before finalizing your decision.

Small Business Financial Facts

According to the SBA, 61.7 million Americans work for small businesses, making up 39.4% of the total private sector payroll. And according to the IRS, 40% of small to midsize businesses file payroll tax returns incorrectly, leading to costly penalties.

PAYROLL TAX OBLIGATIONS

As an employer, you're responsible for filing regular payroll tax returns and making payroll tax deposits. Federal and state payroll tax reports are prepared and filed quarterly (some states may differ). Your company's federal payroll tax deposit schedule for income and employment taxes will depend on the size of those deposits, but it will either be monthly or semi-weekly. The deposits include the federal income taxes, Social Security, and Medicare taxes withheld from employee paychecks and the employer's Social Security and Medicare tax obligations. These taxes get reported quarterly on Form 941, Employer's Quarterly Federal Tax Return.

Federal unemployment taxes (FUTA) get deposited when the amount due exceeds $500. If the FUTA for any quarter comes out to less than $500, that amount will roll forward quarterly until it hits $500. Small employers may end up only making one or two FUTA deposits during the year if they don't hit that threshold every quarter. This tax gets reported annually on Form 940, Employer's Annual Federal Unemployment (FUTA) Tax Return.

The IRS takes employment taxes extra seriously. If you don't pay them on time, in the right amount, and in the right way, your business can be charged stiff penalties. Those penalties will be a percentage of the taxes due, and that percent increases with time, ranging from 2%–15%, plus interest. Penalties are even more severe when it comes to withholding taxes, the taxes you take out of employee pay. These are known as trust fund taxes because your business is holding and submitting those taxes on behalf of your employees. If you don't withhold and remit those on time and properly, you and any other responsible person (like a corporate officer or a payroll manager) could face a Trust Fund Recovery Penalty equal to 100% of that trust fund tax.

YEAR-END DOCUMENTS

If you've ever gotten a paycheck, you've also gotten a Form W-2 to use for your personal tax return. And if you've worked as a contractor, you've probably received Form 1099-NEC from the companies that paid you. Now that you're on the employer side of the relationship, you'll be the one responsible for getting those forms out, along with the required IRS filings that go along with them. Like all things IRS-related, not delivering or filing the forms properly or on time can result in big penalties for your company. To make sure you stay on track, here are some of the federal year-end filings due on January 31 of the next year:

- W-2s and 1099-NECs distributed to recipients.
- W-2s filed with Social Security Administration (SSA).
- Form W-3, a summary of the W-2s filed with SSA.
- 1099-NECs filed with IRS.
- Form 940 filed with IRS.
- Quarterly 941 or annual 944 (depending on your company's filing requirements).

For a complete list of required filings and deadlines, visit the IRS website at www.irs.gov and the state websites for where you have employees. Or, to make your life easier and penalty-free, use a payroll service.

THE RIGHT WAY TO PAY YOURSELF

Hint: It's Not Whatever You Want

Your business provides your income, and it's important to pay yourself the right way. The correct payment method for you depends on your business structure: sole proprietorship, partnership, S corporation, or C corporation. The rules for proprietorships and partnerships are different than the rules for corporations, and it's critical that you pay yourself correctly to avoid potentially severe tax consequences.

LLCs Don't Matter Here

When it comes to paying yourself as a business owner, it doesn't matter if you have an LLC. This business form exists purely for legal reasons, so you'll pay yourself based on the way your business is taxed.

BUSINESS TYPES THAT TAKE OWNER DISTRIBUTIONS

Sole proprietorships and partnerships see very little distinction between the business and the business owners. Though partnerships have more rules as there's more than one person involved, paying yourself works the same way in practice: You simply move money from the business account to your personal account.

In a sole proprietorship, you simply transfer money from the business bank account into your personal bank account or write yourself a check from the company checkbook. This does not have to be done in a set amount or set schedule, but paying yourself regularly can be helpful for budgeting and planning purposes. These payments will *not* have any taxes withheld like a regular paycheck would because, according to tax law, you are not considered an employee of your company. You'll need to make quarterly estimated tax payments to make up for that, so remember to set aside a portion of your profits for income taxes.

In a partnership, you and your partner(s) need to agree on how you'll all be paid. Regular salary-type payments are called guaranteed payments. Extra bonus-type payments are called distributions. Regardless of the type of payment, you will make direct transfers or write checks from the business account to each partner in the agreed-upon amounts. Like with a sole proprietorship, partners are not considered to be employees, so they have no taxes withheld from their pay.

CORPORATION OWNERS ARE EMPLOYEES

As the business owner of a C or S corporation, you are an employee of the business. So, like any job, you need to be on payroll and receive regular paychecks with taxes withheld. The corporation will also pay its share of employer-based taxes, just like it would for any other employee. However, the other portion of owner/employee pay is through nonpayroll distributions, and this tax treatment depends on the type of corporation you have.

S Corporations

S corporations are considered pass-through entities for tax purposes. That means the corporation itself doesn't pay income taxes but rather "passes through" its income to the shareholders (owners) to be reported on their personal tax returns. S corporation shareholders may also take nonpayroll distributions from the company, either by transferring money from the corporation to their personal bank account or writing themselves a check. These distributions would not have any taxes taken out and don't usually generate any extra taxes (unless special circumstances apply—check with your accountant before taking distributions). That's because those distributions have already been taxed as corporate earnings, and since you're paying tax on them regardless, it doesn't matter if you leave them in the corporate account or transfer them to yourself.

But there's a catch: The amount you pay yourself through payroll matters to the IRS. As an S corporation owner, you're required to take "reasonable compensation," and that can be a little tricky to figure out. The reasonable compensation requirement exists because people would be inclined to minimize payroll, which is subject to income *and* employment taxes, and maximize distributions that are only subject to income tax. Payroll gets taxed 15.3% more because of Social Security and Medicare, half paid by the employee through withholding and half paid by the employer. Since technically you're both employee and employer, you foot the entire 15.3% additional tax bill for your payroll.

Reasonable compensation is determined by what you would pay someone else to do that job. It's also based on your company's profits. For example, if reasonable compensation for your job would be $75,000, but your corporation only brought in $60,000 in profits before payroll, it's reasonable to pay yourself a lower salary.

C Corporations

C corporations pay their own income taxes. When shareholders receive extra nonpayroll distributions from the corporation, those are considered dividends, and they are taxable income to the owner/shareholder. They're treated just the same for tax purposes as if you got dividends from a stock investment. So these dividends are subject to *double* taxation: once as regular income to the company then again as dividend income to the shareholder/owner.

This is where reasonable compensation comes into play for C corporation owners/employees. If you're in a high income tax bracket, you may want to pay excessive salaries to avoid double taxation. But if the IRS determines that part of the salary is really "disguised dividends," you could be hit with penalties and interest. As with an S Corporation, "reasonable" is determined by what someone else would earn in the same job elsewhere (a fair salary).

HOW *NOT* TO PAY YOURSELF

Paying yourself the wrong way can cause legal and tax complications. Corporation owners/employees must pay themselves through payroll, while sole proprietors and partners can't.

Do not pay for personal expenses with business funds (for example, using a business credit card at the grocery store). This "commingling of funds" can invalidate the legal separation between you and your business. So, if your business is an LLC or a corporation, doing this can erase the liability protection of the structure. On the tax side, if your business is incorporated, these transactions count as distributions (for S corporations) or dividends (for C corporations) and can cause tax complications.

PROVIDING BENEFITS

Sweetening the Pot

Employee benefits packages include a mix of mandated and optional nonwage offerings provided by the business. These benefits can be used to attract valuable, hardworking employees and keep them happy, especially in a competitive hiring market. Most people immediately jump to health insurance and retirement plans, but there are many more employee benefits you can offer your workers. In addition to benefiting the employees, many of these options result in employer tax deductions or credits that can help save some cash at tax time.

MANDATORY BENEFITS

Both federal and state governments require basic benefits to be provided to employees. Some of these are dependent on the number of employees your company has, while others apply to even the smallest employers. Make sure that you check your state employment laws, as their standards can be stricter than federal laws. Some mandatory employee benefits include:

- Minimum wage: This is the least you can legally pay an hourly employee. The federal minimum wage is set by the Fair Labor Standards Act (FLSA), and states may set their minimum higher than the national requirement.
- Overtime: When employees work more than forty hours per week, the excess is considered overtime, and the mandated overtime

pay rate is 1.5 times their standard wage. States may have their own standards.

- Social Security and Medicare: Employers are required to "match" employee Social Security and Medicare taxes, also called payroll taxes or FICA. Employers must pay a percentage of employee pay for FICA—6.2% for Social Security and 1.45% for Medicare—each pay period, up to the maximum.
- Unemployment: Employees who are laid off or let go (but not fired for cause) are entitled to unemployment benefits for a set time period. Each state determines the amount and period for unemployment benefits.
- Workers' compensation: Employees who get injured or become ill because of their job can receive these insurance benefits. Workers' compensation premiums are paid by employers on behalf of their employees according to individual state regulations.
- Disability: Some states require employers to provide disability insurance coverage for their employees. Disability benefits cover a portion of the employee's salary should they become unable to work for an extended period of time.
- Family and Medical Leave Act (FMLA): This law requires employers with at least fifty employees to provide twelve weeks of parental leave, though it does not require paid leave. Most states have similar laws on the books, including some that require paid leave.
- Consolidated Omnibus Budget Reconciliation Act (COBRA): This federal law requires employers that offer health insurance benefits and have at least twenty employees to make that insurance available to *former* employees and their families for eighteen months. The ex-employee is responsible for paying the plan premiums, but the employer has to facilitate this.

This list covers the basic benefits that all employers are required by law to offer their employees. Employers with more employees may have to offer additional benefits. That said, to attract and retain your ideal employees, you may have to offer unrequired benefits.

Do You Have to Offer Health Insurance?

In the United States under the Affordable Care Act (ACA), employers with fifty or more employees must provide medical coverage to those workers. Small businesses with fewer than fifty employees don't have to offer this benefit. If they choose to, the plan must comply with the ACA.

RETIREMENT PLANS

Small businesses may offer retirement plans, even if you're the only person working for your business right now. Employer-based retirement plans give the owner the opportunity to stash away more money than you can in individual retirement accounts (IRAs). Plus, employer contributions on behalf of employees, as well as the costs to set up and administer, are generally tax deductible to the business. Small business retirement plan options include:

- SEP (Simplified Employee Pension): Good for businesses with a few employees, only the employer contributes to SEPs, up to 25% of each employee's salary with *each* employee getting the same percentage. SEPs are easy to set up, maintain, and require very little paperwork. Each participant gets their own company-funded IRA account.

- SIMPLE (Savings Incentive Match Plan for Employees): These plans are available for employers with no more than one hundred employees. Both employers and employees can contribute. Employers can contribute up to a 3% match to participating employees or 2% for all employees whether or not they contribute. Each participant has their own IRA, and the company must notify each eligible employee annually about: how they can start or change their participation, whether the company will make matching or nonelective contributions, and a summary description of the plan.
- 401(k): Though they require more paperwork than the other plans, these plans allow employees to stash more cash for their futures. Employers have a few options when choosing this type of retirement plan, so talk with an employee benefits expert or your accountant before choosing. Regardless, the employee makes voluntary contributions, and the employer may make matching contributions (some types *require* employer contributions).

Employers starting new retirement plans may be eligible for up to $5,000 of valuable tax credits for three years to offset the costs of administering the plan. The credit is for up to 50% of the plan start-up costs, such as set up, administration, and employee education. You can find out more about the Retirement Plans Startup Costs Credit and more information about the plans themselves on the IRS website at www.irs.gov. Remember: Each type has its own benefits and drawbacks, so talk to your accountant to make the best choice for your business.

HEALTH INSURANCE

If your company has fewer than fifty employees, it's not required by federal law to offer health insurance benefits. That doesn't mean that you can't provide this benefit, which gives your business a leg up when it comes to attracting top talent.

If you offer group health insurance, it will need to be ACA compliant, meeting minimum standards for coverage. Find detailed information about small business healthcare plan options at www.healthcare.gov.

You may also decide to offer group vision or dental benefits for your employees. Depending on the policy details, dental and vision insurance may cover a large variety of preventative and other healthcare.

Most companies have employees pay for a least a portion of these health benefits, so you won't have to foot the entire bill. Don't make the mistake of covering the full cost of premiums, as that will encourage employees who have access to other coverage (like from a parent or spouse) to switch to your plan, bumping up the costs even more.

EXTRA BENEFITS

Along with the "big two" (retirement plans and health insurance), many small businesses offer additional benefits to draw in the best employees. Those extra benefits include things like:

- Paid leave (paid time off, or PTO)
- FSAs (flexible spending accounts) for medical or childcare costs
- HSAs (health savings accounts)

- Life insurance
- Short- and/or long-term disability insurance
- On-site childcare
- Health club memberships
- Meal allowances
- Parking passes
- Remote work options
- Flexible work schedule
- Tuition reimbursement

Most private companies offer some form of PTO, and, as businesses continue to add more competitive benefits, the market is seeing more companies offering flextime and remote work options. These simple benefits can increase the potential employee pool, giving your business access to better employees who'll want to stick around.

WORKING WITH CONSULTANTS AND COACHES

Input from the Outside

As you launch your business, you'll find that you need a lot of support—probably more than you were expecting. There will be gaps in your skills, education, and experience that need to be filled, especially when starting your first small business when you're still learning. From creating action plans to choosing the best tech to identifying key challenges and implementing effective solutions, having qualified help will let you make the best choices for your company.

The solution to your issues may be as simple as bringing in consultants to help you solve process and system issues. Plus, you may benefit from connecting with a business coach to help you work through everything from impostor syndrome to work-life balance issues.

WHAT'S THE DIFFERENCE?

While many people use the ideas of a consultant and coach interchangeably, the two have quite different roles. Coaches help you work *on* your business, while consultants do work *for* your business.

Coaches help business owners overcome issues like fear and impostor syndrome, build entrepreneurial confidence, clarify goals, and identify problems. They act as a combination guide and cheerleader to help you stay on your path toward entrepreneurial success.

Consultants solve problems in the business. They can help design systems and processes, improve efficiency, and supply expertise that you don't currently have in your team. They act for the company, typically working with owners and upper management teams to solve problems and improve profitability.

WORKING WITH COACHES

The best coaches are like mentors, offering direction and support as you take on this enormous job of building your own business. They support your efforts and help guide you on your business-building journey. Research conducted by SCORE found that businesses with mentors were 12% more likely to be in business after a year. Even one interaction with a business coach or mentor can increase your business growth. This long-term relationship will change and grow with you and your business, and the right coach will always have your back.

Here are some key benefits of working with a coach: clarifying your business goals, having an accountability partner, overcoming barriers that are preventing your success, finding a work-life balance, and receiving constant support.

Support can be hard to find when you're starting a small business. Family and friends may resent the time you spend working or your choice giving up a "real" job. And even if they're not pessimistic, they still may not be supportive of your journey as a whole. A coach can fill that support void and keep you motivated when you feel like you're in over your head. That support can guide you from start-up to successful business.

Getting an NDA

Before spilling your business secrets to a coach or consultant, have them sign a nondisclosure agreement, or NDA. These contracts protect your company's sensitive and proprietary information, giving you the peace of mind you need to open the books and share the secrets.

WORKING WITH CONSULTANTS

Consultant relationships tend to be project-based and can be either long- or short-term depending on what you need done. These professionals work to achieve specific goals, such as streamlining tasks or creating more efficient processes for you and your team. You might hire a consultant to help with anything from HR, tech stack, tax planning, legal issues, and more to fill in skill and knowledge gaps without adding full-time staff.

Your business, at least at first, may be too small to have in-house departments to manage specialized types of work. Consultants offer specific expertise to solve problems and design solutions. Since they're not emotionally involved in the company (the way you are), they can offer objective advice—even if it's not what you want to hear.

CHOOSING THE RIGHT PEOPLE

Whether you'll be working with coaches or consultants, it's important to find the right people. You want professionals that you trust and feel comfortable with, who have strong track records and experience working with entrepreneurs in the industry.

With so many small businesses cropping up, the coaching and consulting fields are booming. However, there are a lot of inexperienced people and scam artists out there. That's why you'll really need to vet anyone you plan to work with as a coach or consultant. Pay attention to their experience, education, licenses, and credentials. Look at their website and testimonials, check references, and request a free meet and greet to make sure they're a good fit for you and your company.

Before you start your search for a consultant, have a clear idea of your needs and goals. It's best to create a document with specifics that you can show to the consultants you're considering so they're all working with the same information. How they respond to your document will help you choose the right one for your business.

When looking for a coach, your aims may not be as clear—and that's part of the reason why you'll want to work with a business coach. While qualifications matter here, it's also important that your values align, that you're comfortable being open and honest with them, and that their motivational style works for you.

WHO TO AVOID

It can take a while to find the right consultants and coaches, and many entrepreneurs get discouraged or busy and just hire whoever shows up next. But that can be a mistake. It's crucial to take your time to find the right person to work with. And equally important to know who you absolutely do not want to work with. Here are some red flags to watch out for:

- Someone who comes in with a predetermined plan when they do not yet know the specifics of your business.
- Someone who talks more than they listen and doesn't ask a lot of questions about you and your business.
- Someone who's not interested in how things are being done now.
- Someone who insists on a full fee up front (it's normal to expect a 40%–60% down payment on services).
- Someone who's not responsive when you contact them.
- Someone who doesn't seem to understand your business.
- Someone who doesn't have relevant industry experience.

If you're thinking about working with a professional who ticks more than one of these boxes, consider broadening and continuing your search. For the money you're about to pay, you deserve to work with someone who can propel you and your company forward in a sustainable way. Settling for someone who is unqualified, or doesn't have your business's best interest at heart, is not someone you'll want to work with.

HIRING AND FIRING THE RIGHT WAY

Professional Hellos and Goodbyes

The right employees can make or break your business. That's why it's so important to have a plan and clearly define jobs and expectations before you begin the hiring process. You'll also have to follow some legal guidelines when hiring and firing employees. This process can get overwhelming and complicated for new business owners, so you might want to consider working with an HR (human resources) consultant. These professionals can guide you through the hiring process, screen applicants, develop company policies, and help you develop positive relationships with your staff.

GET SET UP FOR EMPLOYEES

Before you can hire and pay employees, you need to have a plan in place. Your hiring plan will cover how many employees you need, what their roles will be, and how much you can afford to pay them. Remember to include search costs and job posting fees in your budget, as these fees can cost between $1,500 to $2,000 a year on average.

Then there are the logistics that you need to have in place or ready to go before you bring on your company's first hire:

1. Get an Employer ID Number (EIN) from the IRS.
2. Get the state or local ID numbers needed (this varies from state to state).
3. Hire a payroll service.

4. Create an employee handbook.
5. Have all new hires complete Form W-4.
6. Complete Form I-9 for all employees.

Your Employee Handbook

You can find employee handbook templates online. Many payroll providers, such as ADP and Gusto, also offer templates you can use to create your own handbook so you don't have to start from scratch.

POSTING YOUR JOB OPENING

You want to attract quality candidates for your job, and a strong, clear job posting makes that possible. Use a clear job title that candidates can understand, rather than something cute like "marketing guru." Link to your company website and *LinkedIn* profile to assure serious candidates that this is a real job for a real business. Include pointed screening questions to make sure applicants meet the basic requirements for the role.

Once you've got a solid posting, choose the platform you'll use to search for candidates. You should consider posting on the following job boards:

- *Indeed* (www.indeed.com)
- *ZipRecruiter* (www.ziprecruiter.com)
- *LinkedIn* (www.linkedin.com)
- *Monster* (www.monster.com)
- *Handshake* (www.joinhandshake.com)

Once you've received applications, you'll rank and rate them. Most platforms will pre-rank for you based on your screening questions, so you'll have more qualified candidates at the top of the list. From there, you'll create your short list of candidates you'd like to interview.

CONDUCTING INTERVIEWS

Job interviews can be nerve-wracking for new small business owners. Being prepared can help you sail through the process and hire the best employee for the job. Before you conduct interviews, take the time to review each candidate's work history and familiarize yourself with their resumes. Create a list of must-ask questions, including a mix of question types such as open-ended and short answer, that will give you a sense of their character, background, and opinions. Record the interview (with the candidate's permission) or take notes during the process to help you remember important thoughts and details when you compare potential employees later.

You'll also want to allow time for the interviewee to ask questions about the position and the company. As you wrap up, explain next steps to them, such as when they can expect to hear from you. After all the candidates have been interviewed, create a brief summary for each that includes why they would be right for the job and where they might need additional training or support.

Don't Ask Illegal Questions

Several laws exist to protect job candidates from discrimination. They forbid potential employers from asking questions about or relating to topics such as age, family status, gender identity, medical information, religion, citizenship, and disability. Here are examples of illegal questions that may not be obvious at first glance:

- Who takes care of your kids while you're at work?
- Where did you grow up?
- When did you graduate from high school?
- Where does your spouse work?
- How's your health?
- Have you ever been arrested?
- Do you own or rent your home?
- Do you have a bank account?
- How tall are you?

Remember: It's easy to accidentally cross the line, so to stay on the safe side, avoid asking any personal questions during the interview process.

FIRING FOR CAUSE

No matter how careful you are during the hiring process, you'll eventually end up with employees that you need to fire. Maybe they're not a good fit for your team, don't complete tasks properly, or maybe they've done something more serious such as theft. Most US employers are "at-will" employers, meaning they can fire employees at any time without justifying that decision.

Even though you may not need a reason to fire employees, that doesn't mean you can't fire an employee for cause. In this circumstance, the employee would not be eligible for unemployment benefits, which keeps your company's unemployment costs down. Here are ten reasons you can fire an employee for cause:

1. Violating company policy
2. Theft
3. Poor attendance
4. Chronic lateness
5. Damaging company property
6. Insubordination
7. Subpar job performance
8. Falsifying information
9. Having or using drugs or alcohol at work
10. Misconduct

If you plan to fire an employee for cause, make sure that you follow the guidelines in your employee handbook. For example, if it specifies employees will be given warnings before being fired, make sure you give the employee clear notices and document those communications. You may also need to give the employee an opportunity to fix their mistakes before letting them go. But if you must fire them, you may need to write an official termination letter (depending on state requirements), review COBRA options (if the employee participated in a company health plan), and provide a final paycheck. When you don't have an HR department to handle a termination, it's best to have a witness present for the conversation. So, set a meeting for a specific date and time, and make sure to keep things professional, brief, and not open to discussion.

Chapter 5

Reaching Your Ideal Customers

Your business can't sell anything if customers don't know who you are and what you're selling. That's where marketing comes in, introducing you and whatever you're selling to your target audience so they can make informed buying decisions. Marketing combines part education and part persuasion with a dash of excitement mixed in.

Knowing your customers is one of the most important ingredients in small business success. It will be the cornerstone of your marketing, which will drive sales and profits. You'll take a deep dive into their pain points, motivations, avoidances, desires, and fears. This will influence your messaging, or what you say and where you say it. You'll create distinct customer avatars to help focus your marketing messages. Even within your ideal customer pool, people will have different buying behaviors and communication styles. What encourages one to buy may not work for another. With an effective marketing plan in place, you'll find and reach the right customers the right way and help them solve their problems by buying from you.

MARKETING BASICS

The Drawing Board

Marketing is more than just advertising, though many people use the terms interchangeably. It encompasses everything a company does to entice consumers to buy its product or service. To that end, marketing includes advertising along with many other strategies and techniques, such as branding, networking, and customer referrals. Unfortunately, many new businesses take a haphazard approach to their marketing, focusing mainly on advertising rather than developing a well-rounded plan. When you take the time to create a full marketing strategy, your business will reap more benefits than just the next sale.

THE MANY BENEFITS OF MARKETING

While the ultimate goal of marketing is to make sales, that's not the only thing your business will gain from a clear, comprehensive marketing strategy. Along with sales generation and growth, a strong marketing plan can:

- Build an audience of potential customers.
- Create and perfect your brand.
- Boost brand recognition.
- Educate your audience about your company and your product offerings.
- Collect information about your customers.
- Strengthen customer relationships and increase customer retention.
- Help your business stay ahead of the competition.

All of these benefits contribute to your business's ultimate goal: increased revenues. No matter how great your product or service is, customers can only buy from you if they know you exist, and marketing is key to your brand's visibility in an oversaturated market.

THE FOUR PS

The four Ps of marketing—also known as the marketing mix—make up the cornerstone of your sales strategy. This idea goes all the way back to the 1950s when it was coined by Harvard advertising professor Neil Borden, and it's still used widely today. The four Ps include:

- **Product:** This is whatever you plan to sell to your customer, whether it's physical, digital, or a service. Ideally your product will fill a gap in the market or help meet growing consumer demand. Before you can sell your product, you'll need to fully understand what it does and what makes it different and better than similar offerings.
- **Price:** This is how much the product will sell for. When determining pricing, you'll take many factors into account, including the product costs, overhead, and competitor pricing. You'll also consider the opportunity cost of the customer, or the trade-offs they'll have to make to buy your product instead of something else.
- **Place:** This is where customers can buy your product. In addition to whether the product will be sold online or in a physical store or office, place also refers to the product placement. For example, if it's being sold in a store, which shelf will it go on? Will it have a dedicated display? Where and how will it be featured online?

- **Promotion:** This refers to your complete marketing campaign, or how you will communicate with your customers. Promotional activities include advertising, sales promotions (like buy one, get one free), direct marketing, and public relations. It includes promoting you and your business along with the products and services being sold.

Your marketing mix will make use of all four Ps as you develop the right plan for your business.

Marketing by the Numbers

When it comes to marketing, 96% of small businesses include social media in their strategy. E-mail marketing is the most popular tool used by small businesses. And 47% of small business owners run their marketing by themselves.

CREATING YOUR MARKETING STRATEGY

Reaching and communicating with your best customers in a way that translates into sales, especially repeat sales, takes planning. Developing a marketing strategy will take your company further than if you try things at random, hoping something will stick. Here are seven steps that go into creating an effective marketing strategy:

1. Set clear goals: Increased sales may be your end goal, but setting goals along that path will help you get there more quickly. These might include things like building an email list, boosting engagement on social media, or increasing traffic to your website.

2. Determine your marketing budget: The channels (social media, print ads, etc.) you choose for your marketing efforts will, at least partly, depend on how much your business can afford. When spending is limited, you can use less expensive or free options, like sending out press releases or lobbying to be a guest on relevant podcasts.

3. Know your customers: Whatever you're selling has an ideal customer, and it's important that you understand who they are, where they are, and why and how they buy. Once you really know them, you can reach them through the right marketing channels.

4. Assess your competition: Look at how your closest competitors are reaching customers and analyze their messaging. Take note of how your company, product or service, and approach are similar to and different from your competitors, and look for areas where your business has a distinct edge.

5. Craft your message: After you set goals, determine your budget, and know who you're reaching out to, you'll be able to send the right messaging. You'll let potential customers know exactly how they'll benefit by buying your products or services and why you're the best company to buy from.

6. Choose your channels: No matter how compelling your message is, it won't attract customers if it's in the wrong place. It's critical that you choose the right arena for your messaging. That could be regular blog posts on your website, quick hits on social media, in-person meetings at conventions and conferences, or visually stunning print ads. Wherever your ideal customer's eyes are, those are the channels you'll want to emphasize in your marketing.

7. Measure progress: The only way to determine if your marketing strategy is successful is to measure it using key performance indicators, or KPIs. When attempting to view KPIs, you'll want to look at measures that match your strategy—for example, the number of followers, likes, and engagements for social media marketing; unique views and clicks for blog posts; or audience reach and number of inquiries for print ads.

Taking the time to create a complete marketing strategy will help make sure your advertising dollars don't get wasted on the wrong audience in the wrong channels. It will help you hone your messaging so it stands out and shows why what you're selling is unique and desirable as well as how it will improve your customers' lives.

UNDERSTANDING YOUR DREAM CUSTOMERS

What Makes Them Tick...and Buy from Your Business

No matter what products or services your business sells, and no matter how broad their appeal, not everyone will want to buy them. In order for your business to succeed, you'll have to identify the right people: customers who want or need what you're selling *and* also have the inclination and ability to buy it. That group of people is your target market, your dream customers; these are the people you want to reach out to and communicate with. This group is the most likely to buy from you, so you'll want to develop a positive long-term relationship with them. Before you can do that, though, you have to know as much as you can about them.

WHO YOU WANT AND WHO YOU DON'T

A key part of finding your dream customers includes figuring out who you don't want to interact with. This is especially important for service-based business owners, as your work quality can suffer when you're serving a client you don't get along with. When you find clients you love working with, the whole process will be easier, and you'll produce better results. Asking yourself who you most want to work with can help identify your ideal customers and keep you from inadvertently targeting customers you'd rather avoid. You can use these questions as a starting point: If you could work with one particular group of people all the time, who would they be? How could you help them? What value would you add to their lives?

You want to aim for people who will value your products and services and understand that those come at a price they're willing to pay. Customers who constantly find fault, never seem satisfied, or complain about pricing will drain your business. For service providers, clients whose values don't align with yours or whose personalities clash with yours can make your work intolerable. Even when you're first starting out and building your customer list, consider who you don't want on it and specifically avoid marketing to them.

Everyone Means No One

Most new small business owners learn this the hard way: If you create messaging toward everyone, practically no one will respond. Focus instead on reaching the people who actually want what you're selling. A smaller, targeted audience will boost your sales more than millions of uninterested people.

UNDERSTAND THEIR FEARS AND DESIRES

Two of the biggest drivers of buying behavior are fear and desire. People either have a problem that needs to be solved or a need that they want fulfilled. Knowing what motivates your customers can help you interact with them in a more meaningful way. By understanding what they're looking for, you can acknowledge their problem or need and provide your solution. For example, if you're selling bookkeeping services, you can solve the problem of having accurate information at tax time or fill the need of supplying up-to-date numbers for a busy entrepreneur. One message addresses a fear/problem, the other a desire/need. When you know which motivating force drives your potential customers toward buying, it's easier to bring them in.

SEGMENTING YOUR MARKET

Part of nailing down your niche will involve segmenting your market and breaking it down into even smaller, more targeted pieces. For example, if your typical dream customer is a working mom who lives in the suburbs, segments could include things like "and owns a dog," "and drives an SUV," "who works from home," or "who uses more than two streaming services," depending on what you're trying to sell. The segments you choose will relate to your products and services and how this customer can benefit from them. The four most-used ways to segment your market involve:

1. Demographics: Using personal features such as age, marital status, gender, and income.
2. Geography: Based on where customers live or work; this can be as general as a state, or as specific as a street address.
3. Psychographics: Looking at lifestyle, personality, likes, dislikes, attitudes, and interests.
4. Behavior: Specifically buying-related behaviors, such as brand loyalty, stage in the buying journey, how they use products or services, how they make purchase decisions, and why they choose one product over another.

You can create segments based solely on one method or using a combination of them. The more definers you add to the segment, the more targeted your messages can be, and that can lead to more success in influencing customer buying choices. Keep in mind that you *can* target more than one segment; you just wouldn't use the same messaging when reaching out to different segments.

UNDERSTAND WHAT TRIGGERS BUYING DECISIONS

What leads one person to make a purchase may have no effect on someone else, even if both are in your target market. Different customers decide to buy based on their own unique motivators. That said, people tend to make the decision to buy things in four main ways:

1. Impulsive: Spontaneous buyers who want something right now.
2. Methodical: Buyers who do research and need all of the details before purchasing.
3. Emotional: Buyers who commit when they feel a personal connection.
4. Competitive: Buyers who swoop in at the last minute or to collect bonuses.

You'll need to understand the buying habits of your dream customers so you can tailor your messaging and buying process toward those triggers. For example, if you cater to impulsive buyers, you'll want to emphasize "buy now" messaging and make sure to make the buying process as quick and easy as possible. With emotional buyers, you'll need to build a relationship over time through emails, social media, or even through videos and courses before they're ready to purchase.

CREATING YOUR NICHE

Carve Out Your Corner

When it comes to creating a successful business, less is more. No business can be everything for everyone. Without having a specific pool of people to market toward, nothing would be done well, and no one would be happy. A better strategy is to zero in on a niche: a narrow piece of the business and the market. This isn't something you'll just happen upon by happy accident. You'll need to take the time to discover your specialties and hone your business focus. When you find it, your business will gain some distinct advantages, including increased profitability, clear distinction from your competitors, and the ability to excel in your sector.

FOUR KEY BENEFITS OF CREATING A NICHE

While it might seem counterintuitive, focusing your business within a small niche can bring large opportunities for success and profitability. You can use your niche to make your company stand out from its competitors. Choosing a niche doesn't mean you can't add on or branch out in the future. In fact, it can often help determine more profitable ways to increase your offerings. And in the beginning, it can benefit your business in many ways, including these four important areas:

1. Reduces competition: While creating a niche reduces the size of your overall market, it also cuts down on the competition. You'll differentiate your business from companies that cater to

the masses or to other niches inside the broader industry. The customers inside your niche will more easily find your business when they need its products and services.

2. Establishes expertise: By "staying in your lane," you'll be able to build a reputation of excellence and reliability. Building and consistently demonstrating proficiency allows you to establish your business as an expert in the field, easily distinguishing your company from the competition.

3. Inspires customer loyalty: Focusing on a niche allows your company to prioritize quality products and services. Concentrating on excellent customer service and building rapport will help create long-standing customer relationships.

4. Minimizes marketing efforts: It's harder and much more expensive to get new customers than maintain the ones you already have. It's also cheaper, easier, and more effective to market to a very narrow target market.

Finding the right niche will make everything else easier, from marketing to product development, and it will unlock your company's potential for long-term success and profitability.

FROM BROAD FIELD TO NICHE

Your business exists in a field with many competitors, whether you sell books, provide virtual assistance, offer accounting services, or make baked goods. That's your starting point—the broad field that you'll be narrowing down. Get more specific about your company, focusing on particular areas. Consider things like:

- Your strongest skills.
- Tasks you most enjoy doing.
- Your proudest achievements.
- Your strongest problem-solving skills.
- People you prefer to work with.

For example, if you have a virtual assistant business, you may focus on administrative tasks like email monitoring and client communication, marketing tasks like writing and posting content, or business tasks like paying bills and sending invoices. Rather than working with all kinds of businesses, you might narrow it down to acupuncturists, veterinarians, or small book shops. You can also define your niche based on factors like geography, quality, or price. The more specific you get, the more defined your niche will be.

IDENTIFY THE PROBLEMS YOUR BUSINESS WILL SOLVE

Once you've begun to funnel your broad business idea into a smaller niche, you can focus on what you'll be doing to benefit your customers. It's time to identify the specific problems your target customers deal with and figure out whether and how your company can solve them. You'll need to get a sense of your ideal customer's pain points, and the best way to do that is to ask them directly. Create a list of open-ended questions that give those target customers the opportunity to talk about the problems they're facing. You'll begin to see patterns emerge and common problems they face.

If you don't have any potential customers to talk with, you can try visiting online forums where your client base posts. You can search for forums dedicated to your desired niche and read through the discussion chains. Look at the questions people are asking, the answers they're getting, and how that information can help you identify potential pain points. Some good general resources for this include *Alignable*, *LinkedIn*, *Facebook*, *Discord*, and *Reddit*.

RESEARCH YOUR NICHE

Once you've got a sense of what you'd like your business to focus on, it's time to make sure that niche can be profitable and sustainable. This process takes some research and analysis, which will lead to a more clearly defined niche and a sense of how you can make money with it.

First, take a look at the competition. If your chosen niche is supersaturated, you may have to fight harder to get and keep customers. If there's no or very limited competition, it could mean that other companies have learned that this niche isn't profitable, or at least not enough to dive in. Ideally, the niche will have some existing competitors demonstrating that this area can attract enough business to make your venture worthwhile.

Understanding the market for your niche is also key. For your niche to be profitable, the potential market needs to be big enough that your company can make money now and have growth potential for the future too.

Next, check out the population of potential customers. You'll want to develop a deep understanding of their needs, desires, frustrations, and expectations. The more focused your niche, the easier it will be to identify your target customers. If you can't visualize an ideal customer for what you plan to sell, that can signify that you need to redefine your intended niche. It's also important that you can easily reach those customers—a group of great customers that you can't access won't further your sales goals.

Finding Underserved Markets

If you can identify neglected, underserved, or poorly served markets, your niche will have more opportunities for success. You can find these overlooked customers by searching consumer rating websites like *Yelp* or *Trustpilot* to learn what markets are flooded with dissatisfied customers.

ADVERTISING OPTIONS

Getting the Word Out

When it comes to advertising (or distributing your message), you have many options to choose from. For most new small business owners, free and low-cost options seem like the right way to go, but that's not always the case. Some types of businesses should invest in "hard" advertising, using traditional paid media like print or TV ads. Based on your marketing strategy, you'll use a mix of formats, focusing on your customer's preferences.

DIGITAL MARKETING

Digital advertising, also called online marketing, is often the most affordable option for small businesses. There are many ways to advertise in this space, including:

- Email marketing: Collecting or buying email addresses and sending nurture emails (regular messages) to foster loyalty among potential customers. These emails may also be used to notify readers of new products, discounts, and sales.
- Social media posts: Building an online presence through the use of social media platforms. You can create and post regular content and also buy paid ads to get more views.
- Targeted ads: Serving up ads to audiences based on their interests and preferences. Also called behavior-based advertising, these customized ads show up wherever the customer is online, such as on social media and websites they visit.

- Content marketing: Creating blog posts, ebooks, reports, courses, videos, and other downloadable content to build customer relationships. They are often offered for free to serve as lead magnets (a free/special deal in order to collect email addresses) and entice readers to take steps toward an ultimate sale.
- Affiliate marketing: A process where other businesses earn commissions for promoting your products. This revenue-sharing method gives your business more visibility with customers who you wouldn't be able to reach otherwise.

Digital marketing expands your reach without blowing your budget. In-house options such as email marketing, content marketing, and social media posts can be especially effective for building trust and connecting with your core customers.

Search Engine Optimization (SEO)

To get your digital marketing in front of the most eyes, you'll want to maximize SEO techniques that help your content rank higher in search engines like *Google*. This involves using highly searched keywords and tags in your content, attracting people who aren't yet familiar with your business.

MOBILE ADVERTISING

With more people doing everything on their phones and tablets, mobile advertising can get you a lot of bang for your marketing bucks. Technically, mobile advertising is a form of digital advertising but a more specific niche. These ads are specifically designed for and delivered to mobile devices. They can come across as SMS messages, banner ads on mobile-friendly websites, and in-app or in-game ads. Mobile advertising reaches customers right where they spend most of their time and makes taking next steps—like clicking through to make a purchase—easy. Some other benefits of mobile advertising include cost-effectiveness, location-based targeting, shareability (increases the possibility of an ad going viral), immediacy, and personalized messages.

On the downside, different types of cell phones (Androids and iPhones) may use different platforms and app versions. If a user has a negative experience, they can quickly share that as well, triggering negative viral attention. Privacy issues may also come into play, as consumers may feel like mobile ads are intrusive. Before planning your mobile ad campaign, investigate potential legal issues (such as rules for opting in to receive text messages).

DIRECT MAIL

If you've ever gotten "junk mail," you've been a target of direct mail marketing. This includes postcards, catalogs, coupon mailers, and other physical mail pieces, like credit card offers. Though it's not as popular as it once was, this tried-and-true marketing method can work effectively for many kinds of small businesses. It still gets surprisingly high response rates, often higher than email marketing and online display ads.

This marketing tactic can work well for business owners with physical shops, where customers bring the promotional offer they received into the store with them. The tactile experience can be another connection point in the customer relationship. It can also reach more and different potential customers than digital ads, especially if you sell to older demographics who spend less (or no) time online. And since fewer companies use this marketing method, there's less competition in the mailbox than there would be in the inbox.

The downside: The costs of creating, printing, and mailing these pieces can run quite high. You may be able to mitigate some of the costs by avoiding postage in areas that allow these marketing materials to be delivered straight to businesses and residences. (Think about menus shoved under your door, for example.)

RADIO ADVERTISING

If you're trying to reach out to a wide local audience, radio advertising makes a good option. This marketing method is often less expensive than expected, making it cost-effective for small businesses. Customers respond to the repetitive nature of radio ads, so most advertising packages include multiple airings. It's generally more effective to repeatedly run short (fifteen- or thirty-second) ads than to run longer ads fewer times. Running your ads during the same time slots every day ensures that the same people are likely to hear them over and over, increasing the odds that your ad will stick in their heads.

Radio stations tend to have a strong grasp on their demographics— the people who listen to their variety of shows. That gives you direct access to a broader base of your target customers. They also know what they're doing and can help you write, record, and produce your ads.

You can also try to get some free on-air coverage by creating a press release about a major event affecting your business, or participating in or sponsoring a local event.

DECIDING HOW YOU'LL GET PAID

Cash or Credit?

You're in business to make money, and that includes collecting payment from your customers. If you've ever left an online cart because the payment process was annoying, walked out of a store without buying because the checkout lines were too long, or put off paying an invoice because there were no online payment options, you know how a frustrated customer can feel. If these patterns happen with your customers, you could lose sales, not get paid for products or services already provided, or lose repeat business.

You want to make the payment process easy for your customers. The amount they owe should be crystal clear. They should have multiple options for how they can make payments. Plus, they shouldn't have to jump through any hoops in order to pay you. The bottom line is: The easier you make it for customers to pay you, the more likely they will be to buy and the faster they'll pay.

BUSINESS TYPE DICTATES PAYMENT METHODS

The type of business you have will largely determine the payment methods you accept. For example, a retail store won't typically offer a direct bank transfer like Automated Clearing House (ACH) or wire transfers as payment methods. A service business usually won't accept cash payments but may accept all other forms of payment. Here are some general rules for different types of businesses:

- Online sellers use e-commerce platforms like Shopify, payment processors like PayPal and Stripe, credit cards, and debit cards.
- Brick-and-mortar retailers usually accept cash, credit cards, debit cards, and mobile payment apps like Apple Pay.
- Service providers usually accept checks, credit cards, debit cards, ACH, and wire transfers.

Your business must consider whether you have a lot of international sales, average transaction size, transaction volume, and cash flow needs before picking payment options.

OPEN YOUR BUSINESS ACCOUNTS

Before your business can collect payments, it needs somewhere to put them, and that means you'll need to open a business bank account. Even if you're running your business under your own name, you're better off with a separate business account. If you plan to directly accept credit card payments, you'll also need to open a merchant account that can collect credit card payments then transfer the funds into your business bank account.

To open these merchant accounts, your business will need to have its own tax ID number known as an EIN (sometimes FEIN), or employer ID number. The name is a little misleading because you don't have to be an employer to use or need this ID number. If you don't already have one, you can apply online on the IRS website at www.irs.gov.

PAYMENT TIMING MATTERS

When you get paid matters as much as how you get paid, and how much. There may be specific norms in your industry that dictate payment timing. For example, if you have a coffee shop, people expect to pay on-site. If you offer ongoing professional services, customers expect to be invoiced periodically or use autopay. If you work in a project-based business, customers expect to pay a down payment and then make payments until the project is complete. Regardless of industry norms, you can create whatever payment terms you want to, as long as you clearly communicate them to your customers. There are three basic types of payment timing:

- Prepayment: Charging customers before they receive products or services from you—this can be full or partial like a deposit or retainer.
- Point-of-sale: Charging customers at the time of delivery—common with product and in-person service sales (like auto repair or massages).
- Invoicing/delayed payment: Invoicing customers once products or services have been delivered—common with service providers and mixed product/service providers.

Your business may use different methods with different customers or even a combination of methods for a single transaction.

PAYMENT OPTIONS

As a small business owner, you'll want to give your customers choices when it comes to making payments. It's a convenience for them but also facilitates quicker payment for you. You have many payment options that you may offer your customers, but only pick ones that make sense with your business. Choices include cash, checks, credit cards, debit cards, ACH transactions, wire transfer, payment processing platforms, or mobile payment apps (like Apple Pay or Google Pay).

Except for cash, checks, and sometimes ACH transactions, you'll end up losing a portion of payments to fees, usually somewhere between 1%–3%. That's why some companies discourage card payments and wire transfers for higher ticket products and services, preferring to deal with the extra processing time for checks.

The Downside of Cash and Checks

Cash and checks are among the least secure forms of payment, as they can get lost, damaged, or stolen. Checks have the added drawback of potentially bouncing, which can lead to bank charges on top of the lost money from the sale.

ONLINE PAYMENT PLATFORMS

Payment platforms like Stripe, Venmo, and PayPal make payments easier for your customers and collections easier for you. Of course, this comes at a cost with most platforms, usually a small percentage of the amount being paid, which can add up on larger invoices.

If your business uses shopping cart technology or runs on an e-commerce platform, you'll need to make sure these payment platforms can integrate with that software. If you're invoicing clients directly, as long as you have a business account set up on the platform, you can accept payment there.

THE SMART WAY TO EXTEND CREDIT

If you don't collect payment from your customers before or during the sales transaction, you're effectively extending credit. This is common for companies that sell services where you perform the service and then invoice your customer, but it can apply to any type of business. If you plan to work this way, you can set up a simple system to make sure no transactions slip through the cracks and ensure that you will get paid. *Before* you extend credit, you'll want to collect some information about those customers. It's a good idea to run credit checks on customers, but many new business owners feel like they can't afford the fees or risk alienating customers. That said, not getting paid can end up costing your company in the long run. To check credit on an individual customer, you'll need a signed credit application that contains basic information and authorization for you to run the check. Anyone can run a business credit check at any time, as that's public information, but it's still worthwhile having customers complete credit applications too.

Finally, don't forget to send invoices. A lot of small business owners forget this step as they get caught up with other tasks involved in running their companies. An invoice that doesn't get sent to the customer won't get paid. Even if it's been so long that you feel weird sending an old invoice, do it anyway. Every invoice not sent is business you gave away for free even if it was unintentional.

BUILDING CUSTOMER RELATIONSHIPS

The Blocks of a Successful Business

Your company can't exist without customers. And with so many other options for them out there, their relationship with you and your company matters. Positive experiences distinguish you from the competition and keep customers coming back. Your customers' return is crucial to your long-term success, as it's much less expensive to retain existing customers than to attract new ones. Plus, getting new customers while losing old customers won't propel your company's growth as quickly as holding on to both.

Maintaining these relationships will boost your sales and your bottom line, leading to a more successful business. You'll want to take every opportunity to communicate with customers and keep your company in a positive light. That starts with effective customer relationship management.

FIVE KEYS TO IMPROVING CUSTOMER RELATIONS

Even if you have good relationships with all of your existing customers, you can always strengthen those ties. And if those connections could use some attention, there will never be a better time than now to start getting in contact. Here are five important factors to consider when building customer relations:

1. **Connection.** Find ways to connect with your customers, whether that's through shared interests, asking about family, or sharing cute pictures of pets.
2. **Communication.** Let your customers know what's going on with their projects, products, and anything else they pay you for. You'll want to try to answer questions before they're asked and reach out to customers to let them know how important they are.
3. **Share information.** Advertorial content—a mix of editorial, educational, and promotional content—serves a double purpose by educating customers about your products and services in an indirect way.
4. **Follow up.** Check in with prospective and current customers, follow up on proposals to see if prospects have any questions, monitor completed projects to make sure customers are satisfied, and ask for feedback to prove that you care what they think.
5. **Appreciation.** Let your customers know that you appreciate their business, reward them with special discounts or loyalty programs, and send holiday or birthday cards, or even small gifts for referrals.

The key to this relationship is to constantly nurture it. You don't want customers to forget about your company and all it has to offer, or to leave for more attentive competitors. The more your business is on their minds, the more they'll come to you for repeat work and additional purchases.

NURTURE EMAILS

One way you can consistently communicate with your customers is through email. Sending out emails at least every other week, preferably more often, keeps you front of mind. Even when people don't open your emails or take actions based on your messaging, they'll still see your name in their inboxes. This long-term strategy helps build the relationship between you and your customers, and sharing some of your personal experiences (like a story about your dog or recounting a time you were frustrated by poor customer service) helps build that bond. These emails are one-sided conversations, with you talking directly to your customers and asking them to take some kind of action, whether that's visiting your website, using a discount code, or filling out a survey.

As you collect email addresses, you can start to separate customers into targeted lists so you can speak to them more directly. For example, if your business offers pet care services, you might send one email to customers who use grooming services and a different one to customers who use dog-walking services. That way you're talking to clients about what they're interested in, giving them more reason to open your emails.

SOCIAL MEDIA INTERACTION

Connecting with customers through social media can deepen the relationship, especially if you post personal, genuine content mixed in with sales messages. That doesn't mean you need to get deeply personal, just that you'll show them a nonbusiness side of yourself. Maybe you'll occasionally post pictures of your pets, your garden, or yourself outside of work. Share other posts that you like, whether they're about a concert you're dying to see, baby hippos, or Star Wars. The more customers see you as a likable individual, the more trust you'll build.

Respond quickly to comments on your posts, even if just with a like or a laugh. If customers ask questions, answer them whenever possible, or invite them to contact you privately.

You can also engage with your customers' social media. Liking or commenting on their posts gives them another way to connect with you and makes them feel like they matter to you and your business.

CUSTOMER RELATIONSHIP MANAGEMENT (CRM) SYSTEMS

When you start collecting information about your customers, you'll realize there's a lot of it, and it's often stored in several ways. For example, customer contact information may be kept in a different place or system than sales and payment data. That's where CRM software comes in handy—it allows you to collect all of your customer contact information in one convenient tool. Your CRM system will help you track and manage customer interactions, keep contacts organized, and even automate regular tasks (like reminder emails). It will give you a deeper understanding of your customer base and help you segment your list for more targeted communication and marketing efforts.

The best CRM tools include analytics and custom reporting so you can gather important data, like which products or services are selling best to which customer group, or how many customers responded to a specific ad campaign. It can automatically send upsell or cross-sell emails to customers who buy a certain product, re-engage customers who haven't bought recently, or even send coupons to customers on holidays or birthdays.

Some of the easiest, most budget-friendly CRM options for new small businesses include:

- Zoho CRM (www.zoho.com)
- HubSpot (www.hubspot.com)
- Salesforce (www.salesforce.com)
- Pipedrive (www.pipedrive.com)
- Freshsales (www.freshworks.com/crm/sales)

You can start with free trials to see which feels most comfortable for you and your team. Most offer inexpensive plans for newbies and allow you to scale up as your customer base grows.

Upselling and Cross-selling

Upselling is a sales method that encourages a customer to buy an upgraded or premium version of what they intend to buy. Cross-selling suggests similar or related products or services that the customer might want based on what they're buying. Both techniques invite the customer to spend more money while they're already primed to purchase.

Chapter 6

Accounting and Taxes

If you got anxious just reading this chapter title, you're not alone. Business finances are a primary cause of stress for new entrepreneurs, and it often leads to them ignoring the books. That may seem to work for a little while but will cause enormous problems down the road. Even if you're keeping an eye on the bank account and following the balance daily, that won't give you a complete picture of the company finances. And it definitely won't help you prepare for tax time.

Consistent bookkeeping and financial analysis can improve your company's chance of success and profitability. The numbers will provide insights into what's working, what's not, and highlight areas that need improvement to boost profitability and cash flow. Keeping on top of the financial side will help you prevent or quickly spot problems like bank errors, embezzlement, and impending cash shortages. But shoving the bookkeeping to the bottom of the list could land your business in dire financial straits. The good news: It's easier to manage this than you think if you've got the right tools and good support. You don't have to do it alone.

CHOOSE YOUR BOOKKEEPING SYSTEM

Which One Will You (Actually) Use?

No matter what kind of business you have, you need to keep track of the money moving in and out of it. That includes everything from a side gig to working as a freelancer to running an online store. Every transaction has to be tracked and classified in some kind of system, and there are lots of different options you can try. The most important thing is to choose one and use it consistently.

Most bookkeeping software seamlessly imports transactions from bank and credit card accounts, and many can also manage app transactions (such as Square and Stripe). That doesn't mean your books will be automatically up-to-date and correct all the time. You'll still need to put in some effort to keep the information flowing and properly managed.

START WITH DEDICATED BUSINESS ACCOUNTS

Having separate bank, credit card, and payment platform (like PayPal and Venmo) accounts for your business is a simple way to make your bookkeeping tasks much easier. You know everything flowing through those accounts is business-related. When you mix business and personal accounts, you burden yourself with the extra task of having to sort through every transaction to figure out which goes where. Eliminating that burden will make your business bookkeeping go much more smoothly.

On top of that, though, if your business is an LLC or a corporation, it's crucial to keep business and personal money strictly separate. Failing to do so can result in losing the legal liability protection of the entity.

STICKING WITH SPREADSHEETS

Some people love tracking information in spreadsheets. It takes some extra work to develop the format, templates, and macros, but it also gives extra control over the way the information gets processed. Microsoft Excel has some preloaded customizable templates that can help you get started. This program also allows you to do more complex calculations than standard bookkeeping software, as well as more options for creating tables and graphs.

Some tips for keeping your books strictly in spreadsheets:

- Your first spreadsheet should be a chart of accounts, a listing of all the accounts your business will use to categorize transactions.
- Download your bank, payment platform, and credit card statements as CSV files for easy importing.
- Create a sheet that tracks customer invoices and payments, so you'll know at a glance how much is outstanding.
- Start with spreadsheet templates to create your company's financial statements.

This method can work well for small businesses with relatively few transactions, at whatever number is manageable for you on a weekly basis (or more frequently). It can get unwieldy when the number of transactions grows, leading to errors and missed transactions, especially if you don't keep up with it and regularly reconcile your accounts. You'll have problems if your customers don't get invoiced and your vendors don't get paid. So, if you plan to use spreadsheets to track your business finances, you'll need to commit to processing and tracking transactions regularly.

BASIC BOOKKEEPING SOFTWARE AND APPS

Bookkeeping software offers huge advantages over trying to keep up with the accounting manually or using spreadsheets. Key benefits include:

- Automated processes, like importing bank feeds or sending recurring invoices.
- Easy transaction management and organization.
- On-demand reporting.
- Customer invoicing and invoice tracking.
- Tracking vendor bills and payments.
- Real-time, more accurate financial information.

Most accounting software and apps include these basics, and some also include extras like project management and time tracking. There are free options available, but most businesses quickly outgrow those and need the paid versions to keep track of all their transactions. The best and most user-friendly bookkeeping software options include user tutorials, extensive learning libraries, and easy navigation. Most have different pricing levels, so you can start with the most basic and move up as your business needs more functionality. Plus, most offer a free thirty-day trial period, so you can test-drive a few options to see which feels most comfortable for you. Popular options include QuickBooks, FreshBooks, Zoho Books, and Xero.

Whichever software you choose, make sure to set it up correctly. Many of the initial setup features can't be undone, so if you're unsure, get help. Once it's ready to go, keep up with the transaction processing. The software can't benefit your business if you don't actively use it.

TRACKING INVENTORY

Good inventory management can be the difference between success and failure for a small business, and you can't manage inventory if you're not tracking it. It's crucial for that information to be accurate and current no matter what kind of products you're selling. Some small business owners may prefer to track their inventory manually; others will go straight for inventory-management software and apps. Whichever method you choose, it will start with an inventory ledger, or a complete record of every inventory-related transaction, such as a purchase or sale.

If you plan to go the manual route, using a notebook or a spreadsheet, you'll set up your ledger so you can record transactions in it as they happen. A good inventory ledger will have columns for:

- Transaction date
- Product name and description
- Transaction type
- Quantity
- Unit cost (for a purchase) or price (for a sale)
- Total cost or price
- Running quantity balance

For manual systems, it's easiest to have a separate ledger page for each inventory item. For example, one page for puzzles, one for board games, one for action figures, and so on. Going manual can work if your business has low-volume sales (like just selling a few big-ticket items every day) but will quickly become unmanageable if you sell a lot of items.

For those businesses that have (or anticipate having) higher sales volumes, bookkeeping programs can help with inventory management too. Many bookkeeping programs include basic inventory tracking or have add-on modules for more sophisticated tracking needs. They typically also integrate with POS systems for easier data management.

Point of Sale (POS) Systems

If you've ever checked out at the grocery store, you've used a POS system. This set of devices (like card readers) and software allows merchants to make in-person sales and collect payment from customers instantly.

KEEP YOUR BOOKS CURRENT AND CORRECT

Mind the Money

If you don't know how your business is doing, you can't move it forward. And you won't have a clue what's going on in the business if you don't keep up with the bookkeeping. You can't pull financial statements for potential lenders or investors. You can't tell whether you'll be able to make payroll next week. You won't know if your business is running at a profit or loss. In short, you'll be operating blindfolded and making decisions in the dark.

From getting taxes right to realistic revenue forecasting to avoiding overdrafts, accurate accounting will keep your business on track. Without correct and up-to-date numbers, you cannot properly run your business. But when you stay on top of the books, you'll be in a better position to improve cash flow, increase profits, and position your business for sustainable growth.

WHAT HAPPENS WHEN YOUR BOOKS ARE BEHIND?

For a successful business, it's crucial to be consistent with your bookkeeping. It's easy to let this task slide, especially if you find it boring, confusing, or overwhelming. Ignoring the books will just make your financial situation worse and position your company for failure.

Here are ten serious consequences your business will face if the books aren't kept up-to-date:

1. You won't be able to make reasonably accurate estimated tax payments.
2. You'll lose out on valuable information and planning opportunities.
3. Bills won't get paid on time.
4. Customer invoices won't get sent.
5. You won't notice when customer invoices go unpaid.
6. Some transactions will get missed, distorting the P&L (Profit and Loss) Statement.
7. You may inadvertently overdraw bank accounts or go over the limit on credit cards.
8. You won't know if your business is operating at a profit or loss.
9. The business could run out of (or accidentally overstock) inventory.
10. You won't be able to plan or budget effectively.

This list could go on and on, as these are just some of the major problems with ignoring your books. So, if you can't (or don't want to) manage the business books yourself, find someone else to do it. Reaping the benefits of up-to-date books and avoiding the potential pitfalls of not keeping them current are well worth the time and cost.

RECONCILE REGULARLY

Reconciling accounts means making sure that the account balance in your books matches external documentation, like a bank or credit card statement, a loan statement, or a POS report. A lot of small business owners skip this step, but that can be a costly mistake. Staying on top of the reconciliation process helps make sure that:

- All transactions are accounted for (e.g., banking fees and credit card finance charges).
- No transactions have been double counted, which happens more often than you'd think with automatic banking feeds in bookkeeping software.
- No erroneous or fraudulent transactions are on the statement.
- The interest portion of loan payments gets properly accounted for.
- All your account balances are verified in case of an audit.

What can happen when accounts aren't reconciled regularly? You could overlook bank fees and end up overdrawn, bouncing payroll checks and payments to vendors. Credit card fees—like financing, over limit, and late payment charges—could pile up and bring the balance up to (or over) the limit. Unreported fraudulent or erroneous charges could be past the reporting date, meaning you won't be able to recover the lost money from the bank. Any of these examples could cost your business money. And some can also lead to strained relationships with vendors, employees, and other stakeholders.

COMPANY CASH FLOW DEPENDS ON ACCURATE BOOKKEEPING

In the beginning, cash is what your business needs to stay alive. It's more important than profitability because your company cannot operate without money. And when money is tight, as it typically is for start-ups, knowing your current cash situation to the dollar can mean the difference between staying afloat or going out of business.

Checking the balance in the bank isn't enough. You have to account for money going out to vendors and employees, money coming in from customers, and figuring out how to deal with the difference. Even if you have a stockpile of cash from lenders or investors, it won't last as long as you need it to without careful management.

KEEPING TRACK OF INVENTORY

If your business sells products, accurately accounting for inventory will be a critical part of your success. You need to always know how much of which items you have on hand, which are running low, and which are at risk for spoiling. You can't manage your inventory if it's not properly accounted for, so prioritize keeping track of this valuable asset.

The easiest solution is an effective POS (point-of-sale) system to form the cornerstone of your inventory tracking system. A complete POS system works on the sales side of inventory, effortlessly tracking a wealth of information in real time. From scanning barcodes to processing card payments to creating receipts, these systems make the checkout process a snap even for high-volume businesses.

POS systems can track a lot of data for you, such as:

- Customer information
- Details for items sold (such as description, quantity, and price)
- Transaction date and time
- Product barcode (such as UPC or SKU)
- Item price
- Current inventory levels
- Minimum inventory levels

Most systems allow you to pull a wide variety of analytical reports, including custom reports, so you can better understand how inventory is moving in and out of your business. Popular small business POS systems include Square, Vend, and Lightspeed.

Regardless of how you decide to track inventory, you'll need to conduct physical counts at least annually to make sure the numbers in the computer match the inventory you actually have. Yes, physical inventory counts are boring and time-consuming, but they're critical for accurate tax reporting and let you identify and reconcile any discrepancies.

Inventory Shrinkage

When you have fewer products on hand than in your inventory tracking system, you have shrinkage. Shrinkage can be the result of clerical errors or actual inventory losses. Losses may involve theft or damage to inventory that makes it unsellable.

UNDERSTANDING THE NUMBERS

Subtract the Stress from Bookkeeping

Having accurate, up-to-date numbers is step one for managing your business's bookkeeping. Understanding the numbers comes next, and it can be equally (maybe even more) important to your current and future business success. By understanding the numbers in your business accounts and beyond, you can make informed decisions about your company. Throughout owning your business, you'll learn, for example, which products are most profitable, which expenses could be cut back, and how much you can pay yourself without sabotaging the company.

Accounting results give you vital information about your company's financial health and offer direction for future growth and increased profitability. If you don't know what you're looking at, you won't be able to steer in the right direction or evaluate the company's performance. Your decisions won't be based on the facts, and that can lead to serious financial problems. At the end of the day, it's vital to learn how to read and analyze your numbers so you can make the right choices for your business.

THE BIG SIX ACCOUNTS

In accounting, you have accounts, or categories that collect all the financial information about a particular item. There are six kinds of main accounts:

1. **Assets.** These are permanent things the business has, such as computers, chairs, machinery, and cash. The asset category usually gets separated into two groups: current assets, which

can convert into cash within one year, and long-term (or fixed) assets that your company will use for a long time. Current assets include things like inventory, accounts receivable (or what customers owe you), and cash. Fixed assets include office furniture, patents, and vehicles.

2. **Liabilities.** These are what the business owes, including credit cards and loans. They are usually separated into current liabilities (due within one year) and long-term liabilities. Current liabilities include vendor invoices and credit card balances. Long-term liabilities include bank loans and mortgages.

3. **Equity.** This term describes the ownership of the company, or the difference between assets and liabilities. The type of equity depends on business structure. Sole proprietorships have owner's equity, partnerships have partners' equity, and corporations have shareholders' equity.

4. **Revenues.** These are sales, or money the company brings in by selling its products and services.

5. **Cost of goods sold (COGS).** This includes what the company paid for the products it resells.

6. **Expenses.** This means the normal costs of doing business, such as insurance, payroll, rent, and office supplies.

Each of the main accounts gets broken down into more detailed subaccounts. For example, checking account, office furniture, and accounts receivable (what customers owe you) all fit under the asset umbrella. This structure helps organize transactions so you can more easily understand the company finances.

Are COGS Expenses?

Cost of goods sold is a type of expense, but it's held separately from others because you can directly connect it to product sales. For example, if you buy books to resell to customers, those same books become COGS once they've been sold. If you buy books to use for training employees, those books count as expenses because they aren't being resold.

THREE MAIN REPORTS

In accounting, there are three key business reports every entrepreneur should be familiar with: a balance sheet, a profit and loss statement (P&L), and a statement of cash flows.

These reports work individually and together to give you important data about your company's financial health. While many small business owners focus firmly on the P&L, the other two reports provide valuable information that you can use to improve profitability, cash management, and business success.

BALANCE SHEET

A balance sheet is a snapshot of the company's assets, liabilities, and equity at a specific point in time: the date of the report. It's formatted in those three main sections, with each broken down into more detail to show you the status of every account. This report shows you what you as the business owner would have left if you liquidated all of the company assets and paid of all the liabilities.

The balance sheet gives you a clear picture of how much debt the company has and who it owes. It also shows how much cash is available right now and how much will be coming in through accounts receivable (the amount your customers owe you). You can look at comparative balance sheets from different time periods to see the company's financial progress.

The Accounting Equation

The accounting equation is the foundation of balanced bookkeeping: assets equal liabilities plus equity. This is represented on the balance sheet. It shows how much of the company is owned rather than owed. It's sort of like a house with a mortgage where the house is the asset, the mortgage is the liability, and the equity is how much of the house you own.

PROFIT AND LOSS STATEMENT

The P&L shows your revenues, COGS, expenses, and profit or loss over a period of time. For example, a P&L could cover a month, a quarter, or a year. It starts with revenues then deducts COGS to come up with the gross profit (the amount that product sales exceeded the costs of those products to the company). The next section lists all of the operating expenses from advertising to legal fees to travel. The total expenses get subtracted from the gross profit to show your net profit (or loss)—your bottom line.

STATEMENT OF CASH FLOWS

Also called a cash flow statement, this report breaks down three different ways money moves into and out of the business:

1. Operations: Through regular business transactions, revenues in and expenses out.
2. Borrowing: Loan proceeds coming in and loan payments going out.
3. Financing: Owners contributing money to the business and pulling money out of it.

With this report, you can see clearly where the money that's keeping your business afloat is coming from. In the beginning, you'll probably rely heavily on borrowing and financing activities. For your business to succeed, most of the cash will need to come from operating activities.

UNDERSTANDING CASH FLOW AND PROFITS (AND HOW TO HAVE BOTH)

Show Me the Money!

A lot of new business owners get confused by the disconnect between profits and cash. It's weird to think the bank account could be full of money, but the company is operating at a loss. Or that the company is wildly profitable, at least on paper, but the bank balance is frighteningly small.

A healthy business has plenty of profits and cash, but it can take some time to build both. By focusing on each individually, you'll have an easier time increasing both. That's because the steps needed to boost cash are different from the steps needed to boost profits. Sometimes they work in opposition, so you'll have to prioritize. And while the instinct is to put profits first, no business can survive without cash—cash is the higher priority.

CASH FLOW FROM AN ACCOUNTING PERSPECTIVE

Cash flow describes the way money moves into and out of your business. That cash can come from or go to three main activities: operations, investing, and financing. In the beginning, for most small businesses, cash comes from the financing section, but the goal is to generate positive cash flow primarily from operations.

Operations encompasses sales and expenditures, the everyday money moving in and out during the normal course of business. Increasing sales doesn't always increase cash flow due to invoicing and payment delays. On the other hand, reducing expenses often increases cash flow, even if not immediately, but it can lead to difficulty operating the company if they're cut too deeply.

Investing activities refer to investments made by your business, such as asset purchases. This would include buying things like delivery trucks, an office building, or computer equipment and software. If you later sell those assets, the cash coming in would go in this section. Most small businesses will have minimal investing activity.

Financing activities include loans and investments *into* the business. For example, it includes the money you and other owners (such as partners or shareholders) put into the company or loan proceeds received from a bank. It would also include money that you (as the owner) have loaned the company and expect to be paid back, as well as payments back to other owners in the form of dividends or distributions. This section covers both getting money from lenders, such as vendors and credit card companies, and paying money back to them. It also includes money flowing back to owners in the form of dividends or distributions.

Where Do Grants Go for Cash Flow?

In most circumstances, grants would go in the operations section of the statement of cash flows. They're generally considered to be revenue and are often taxed, at least by the federal government. And they're often earmarked to cover operating expenses.

PROFITS (OR LOSSES) ON PAPER

Profits, or net income, come from a simple math formula: revenues minus expenses equals profits, or losses if the result is negative. This tells you whether your business is bringing in enough revenue to cover all of the operating costs. It's normal for a new business to be running at a loss for a while. It takes time to build a customer base and generate enough sales to outweigh the business expenses.

Your business can show profits with or without having enough cash on hand. That's because profits may include some noncash transactions that affect the bottom line, such as:

- Accounts receivable: Invoicing customer accounts for goods and services sold to them for which payment has not yet been received.
- Depreciation: An accounting method of expensing an asset slowly over time; for example, expensing a $10,000 machine for $1,000 per year over ten years instead of paying in full at the time of purchase.
- Accrued interest income: Recording interest that has been earned, such as on a CD (certificate of deposit) or an investment bond, but not yet received as cash.
- Prepaid expenses: Recording expenses as they are actually used rather than when they get paid, for example, paying a six-month insurance premium in January and spreading the expense evenly through June.
- Accrued expenses: Recording the purchase of goods or services used by the business but not yet paid for, such as year-end bonuses paid out in the following calendar year.

Most of these transactions will eventually involve cash but not at the time the transaction has been recorded. All of these will affect the profits on paper without having any current impact on cash.

FIVE WAYS TO IMPROVE BUSINESS CASH FLOW

There are effective, simple steps you can take to improve your company's cash flow without decimating your profits. Some of them may hurt profits slightly and temporarily, but they can be easily altered once the incoming cash flow becomes steadier. All of these methods can be implemented quickly to help boost cash as quickly as possible:

1. Invoice customers *immediately*. They can't pay you if you haven't billed them.
2. Offer early-payment discounts. Let customers know that if they pay you within five days (or three or ten, whatever works for your business) they'll get a small discount, usually around 2%–5%.
3. Make it easy for customers to pay. Offer as many payment options as possible, including credit cards and payment processors like PayPal, even if you'll pay a small percentage of your revenue in processing fees.
4. Reduce unnecessary spending. Any expense that is not essential for keeping the lights on can wait until you have more cash available.
5. Delay vendor payments. If your vendor offers thirty-day payment terms, don't pay them sooner, even if you'll lose out on a discount, because right now cash flow is more important.

Longer term strategies include focusing on more efficient inventory management, parking any extra cash into high-yield savings accounts, and leasing assets (like trucks or production equipment) instead of buying them outright.

HIRING A BOOKKEEPER

Please, Just Handle This for Me

For almost all small businesses, the answer to the question of "should I hire a bookkeeper?" is "absolutely, yes." While bookkeeping seems easy, especially when you're using dedicated software, it's very easy to mess up if you don't really understand accounting principles. And while most business owners think they'll have time to deal with the company books, they just don't—it's the task that always gets shoved to the bottom of the to-do list. That idea of moving financial tasks down in priority can cause a lot of problems, both year-round and at tax time.

TEN BENEFITS OF HIRING A BOOKKEEPER

Most small business owners start out trying to manage the books themselves. When they finally hire someone else to handle it, they always wish they'd done it sooner. Having someone to take care of the bookkeeping, whether you take on an employee or use a professional, will benefit your company in many tangible ways. Here are the ten biggest benefits of hiring a bookkeeper:

1. Your books will be up-to-date.
2. Customers will be invoiced promptly.
3. Unpaid customer invoices won't slip through the cracks.
4. Accounts will be reconciled regularly to catch unrecorded payments and receipts.

5. Bills will get paid on time.
6. You won't be overwhelmed by all of the financial details.
7. You'll be ready for tax time without a last-minute crunch.
8. You'll have another perspective on the business finances.
9. Your company will save money by avoiding late fees and catching errors quickly.
10. You'll be free to focus fully on your business and take more time for yourself outside of working hours.

Your bookkeeper will keep things organized and current. They will help your business thrive and get you back to doing the parts of your business you're most passionate about. Plus, if you're curious about the finances, you'll be able to pull reports from your accounting software and know that they're accurate. All of these factors together give you valuable planning and budgeting information that will help propel your business forward.

Bookkeeper versus Accountant

What's the difference between bookkeepers and accountants? Bookkeepers record and process daily transactions and may handle things like invoicing and bill payments. Accountants analyze the financial information to offer insights and strategies for improving business operations.

THE COSTS OF YEAR-END CLEANUPS

All year long you meant to get a handle on the bookkeeping for your business, but it just never happened. So, at year-end, you're suddenly facing a mountain of transactions to deal with, and you're not quite sure if you're processing them correctly. Your tax professional needs the numbers to file your tax return, so you feel the pressure to get it done. Long story short, you reach out to some accountants or bookkeepers to see how much a year-end cleanup will cost you. The fee surprises you, and it's not in a good way. These end-of-year jobs typically start at $2,500 or more, and depending on the shape of your books and your transaction volume, the bill could end up costing even more.

As if that wasn't expensive enough, paying an accountant to do your year-end cleanup is not the only cost here. By not keeping your books up-to-date and correct all year long, you may have:

- Not invoiced all customers for all products or services provided.
- Overlooked unpaid customer invoices and now feel like it's too late to remind them.
- Not had a sense of your eventual tax bill so you could make proper estimated tax payments.
- Not realized a bank or credit card statement had mistakes on it.
- Not known how your business was performing.
- Overdrawn bank accounts or gone over the limits on credit cards.

Issues like these can all affect your company's cash flow and profitability, even to the point of putting you out of business. When you keep your books up-to-date and correct, you can catch these problems and solve them as they arise, or even avoid them all together.

HIRING THE RIGHT BOOKKEEPER

When you decide to hire someone to take care of your business books, the first step is figuring out whether you want to outsource to an accountant or bring someone on board to manage them in-house. Most new small businesses don't have the financial capacity to hire a dedicated bookkeeping employee, so they end up using bookkeeping service firms, freelance or virtual bookkeepers, or their accountant's firm. Once your business grows to the point that you have dozens of employees and annual revenues in the millions, a full-time in-house bookkeeper will make more sense. In the meantime, outsourcing will be a more cost-efficient choice.

Any bookkeeper you consider working with should have at least 3–5 years of experience managing small business books, preferably in your industry. Most bookkeeping software companies offer certification programs for professionals, demonstrating their proficiency. It's also important that you feel comfortable with the person taking care of your business books.

You can search for freelance bookkeepers on sites like *Upwork* (www.upwork.com) and *Indeed* (www.indeed.com). You can also search for local bookkeepers in your area. Of course, there are also online bookkeeping firms like Bench (https://bench.co) or Bookkeeper360 (www.bookkeeper360.com) as options.

Using an accounting firm for bookkeeping services may be more expensive than other options, but you'll get what you're paying for. In addition to the transaction processing, you'll get planning and financial management guidance. Plus, they'll already have your complete, accurate books at tax time, so you won't have to worry about getting the information to them.

INCOME TAXES DEPEND ON BUSINESS STRUCTURE

Stay Ahead of the IRS

How your business reports and pays taxes depends wholly on the business structure. The IRS treats some forms of business, such as sole proprietorships, as if they don't exist and others, like C corporations, as if they were independent people. Some companies will file their own income tax returns and pay their own taxes. Others will file "just information" tax returns while the owners personally pay tax on the business income. A third business type will include the company tax return inside its owner's personal tax return.

It's important to know which type of tax return your business has to file and when it's due. Most new small business owners will benefit greatly from having a professional preparer do the taxes, especially for the first year. The risks of getting a tax return wrong if you DIY are pretty high and often result in you or your business reporting income incorrectly, paying the wrong amount of taxes, or missing key filing dates. Before you take on this nerve-wracking task yourself, you'll want to make sure you understand exactly what needs to be done.

SOLE PROPRIETORSHIPS

The tax return for a sole proprietorship is part of the owner's tax return. The income and expenses get reported on Schedule C: Profit or Loss from Business (Sole Proprietorship). In addition to that information, Schedule C asks for:

- The business tax ID (if it's different than your Social Security number).
- A brief description of the type of business: What you do and sell.
- The appropriate NAICS code (to categorize your business).
- The accounting method: Cash or accrual basis.
- Whether the business paid any contract workers.
- Whether you filed 1099s for any contractors.
- Whether you materially participated in the business (which determines if business losses may be tax-deductible).

There's also a section for business use of your personal vehicle, so you can deduct those related expenses as well. If you work from home and want to deduct home office expenses, you'll also include Form 8829 to report that information. If your business had a profit of at least $400, you'll also need to complete Schedule SE to calculate your self-employment taxes.

What's Your NAICS?

The US Census Bureau uses the North American Industry Classification System (NAICS) to collect, analyze, and report statistical data about businesses in the United States. These six-digit codes provide information about the high-level business sector, industry group, and specific industry for each company. You can find more information including a complete list of codes at www.census.gov.

PARTNERSHIPS

For tax purposes, partnerships file information returns on Form 1065, but they don't pay any taxes on their income. The return includes a special form called Schedule K-1 that details each partner's share of income, losses, and more. The actual business income passes through to the individual partners and gets reported and taxed on their personal returns.

Partners who work for the business will also pay self-employment taxes on their share of company profits, whether or not they take any money (or other assets) out of the business to pay themselves. Regular salary-type payments to partners are called guaranteed payments. Other payments to partners are called distributions, and they are limited to the partner's current ownership portion of the business.

Partnership tax returns are due on March 15, a month before personal tax returns, so that the partners in a business each have enough time to file their personal taxes. The Schedule K-1 gets distributed when the return is filed, giving each partner the information they need to properly report their income.

S CORPORATIONS

S corporations file annual information returns on Form 1120-S but, like partnerships, don't pay taxes on their income; the return also includes a Schedule K-1. Each shareholder reports their portion of corporate profits on their personal tax return.

Shareholders who work for the corporation must be on the payroll and receive "reasonable compensation" (an IRS term) for their work. Those paychecks will have taxes taken out just as if the shareholders worked for any other employer, and all payroll expenses are deductible for the corporation. Salaries must be paid to a shareholder before that shareholder can take other distributions (a.k.a. payments to themselves, not through payroll).

C CORPORATIONS

C corporations file their own tax returns on Form 1120 and pay taxes on their income. These corporate returns include an IRS version of a profit and loss statement and a balance sheet. The corporation reports its gains, losses, deductions, and credits, then pays any income taxes due out of corporate funds.

Unlike other business forms, distributions—called dividends—from C corporations to their shareholders get taxed twice. That's because they're paid out with funds the corporation has already paid income tax on. The shareholders receiving these dividends have to report them on their personal tax returns as income, just the same way they would if they invested in any stock that paid out dividends.

LLCs Don't Count for Taxes

LLCs don't exist in the eyes of the tax code. Their tax situation is based on the tax structure of the company. A single member LLC gets taxed as a sole proprietorship, a multi-member LLC as a partnership, and an LLC that has elected to be taxed as an S or C corporation files based on that election.

ESTIMATED TAX PAYMENTS

Anyone who has a federal or state income tax burden needs to make payments throughout the year. When you're an employee, income taxes are withheld from your gross pay and remitted to the IRS on your behalf. Business owners and C corporations must proactively make those payments through quarterly estimated tax payments.

It can be tricky to figure out what the eventual tax bill will be for the year and make appropriate estimated tax payments, especially for a brand new business. The IRS requires four equal payments that come to at least 90% of the total tax that will be due. When your business is a pass-through entity, where the business income appears on your personal tax return, this gets further complicated by other income sources you may have. If you don't pay enough each quarter or pay late, you could be hit with IRS penalties and interest. So, it's in your best interest to consult a tax professional to help you get your tax numbers as close to accurate as possible.

SALES TAX CAN GET COMPLICATED

Tricky Transactions

Sales tax is a levy based on a percentage of a sale that gets added to the total and collected from the customer. That collected sales tax then gets remitted to the taxing state or locality. Your business acts as the middleman here, collecting sales tax from customers and then sending it along to the government. The business is legally obligated to collect, report, and remit sales tax. The sales tax itself doesn't cost your business any money, but processing and managing it properly will.

States control sales taxes, and that means there are fifty different sets of rules that you have to follow and rates that you have to charge. Some states only tax physical products; others tax services and digital products. Some states require sales tax collection based on where the business is located, others based on where the customer is. On top of that, some localities within states have their own sales tax rules. And some states don't have sales taxes at all. You'll need to figure out the rules for whichever states and localities your company deals with, and that can be especially tricky for online sellers.

UNDERSTANDING NEXUS

The first lesson of sales tax involves a concept called nexus. In sales tax terms, nexus refers to the business connection between a state and a seller. Sounds simple, but it quickly starts to feel like getting lost in a maze. Each state has different nexus requirements, which are usually based on physical presence or economic nexus.

Physical presence can mean anything from having a store, warehouse, or office building in a state, to selling products at a single trade show, to having a remote part-time employee who lives there. Economic nexus may be based on a dollar threshold, number of sales transactions, or a combination of both conducted in a state.

For example, if you sell products online to customers all over the United States, you could have sales tax nexus in multiple states depending on those states' requirements. That would be in addition to any state where your business has a physical presence. It's up to you to figure out where your business has sales tax nexus, apply for a seller's permit there, and begin collecting and remitting sales tax. Make sure to get that permit and your company's sales tax ID before you start selling.

Where to Find State Sales Tax Rules

You can find each state's sales tax laws on that state's website, and you can find links for all fifty states on the IRS website at www.irs.gov. You can also find summary information on sites like *The Tax Foundation* (www.taxfoundation.org).

SOME PRODUCTS AREN'T TAXABLE

As if sales tax wasn't confusing enough, some products are exempt from sales tax (again, depending on state and local laws). Generally, necessities like clothes, food, and medicine are exempt from sales tax, but that's not true in every state and locality. Even inside those aforementioned categories, some items may be subject to taxes. For example, prepared foods may be subject to sales tax even if food is otherwise nontaxable in the state.

In addition, if goods are being purchased for resale, your company doesn't have to collect the sales tax. That's the job of the reseller, because sales taxes are imposed on the *final* customer of the product. For example, if your company sells fifty books to another bookstore that ran out of stock, you wouldn't have to collect any sales tax. As long as the customer provides you with a valid resale certificate, the sales tax is not your problem.

DIFFERENT RULES FOR ONLINE SELLERS

If your business sells online, the rules for collecting sales tax are different. As a "remote seller," you could be responsible for charging, collecting, and remitting sales tax where the customer receives delivery. That's true regardless of the sales tax rules in the states where your business has a physical presence. You'll have to register in every state where your company is selling products *before* you can start collecting the sales tax. You'll also have to keep track of each state and locality's sales tax rates to charge customers the proper amount.

The economic nexus thresholds for each state vary, but they start at $100,000 in sales (in that state) or two hundred transactions. So, you may not hit nexus requirements in your first few months in business, but that can quickly change as your business grows. Keeping an eye on this can help you avoid fines and penalties for failure to collect or report sales taxes—and that can really add up when multiple states are involved.

SALES TAX SOFTWARE AND PLUG-INS

Sales tax is not something you want to deal with manually, especially if your business has any online sales. Luckily, there are several software and plug-in options available to take the burden of figuring out sales taxes off your shoulders.

Some sales platforms, like Etsy and eBay, take care of sales tax in their roles as "marketplace facilitators," though in some states your business may also be required to submit sales tax returns. Others, like Shopify, don't deal directly with sales tax but make it easy for you to automate sales tax collection.

Popular sales tax software and plug-ins (that work in connection with your sales platform) include:

- Avalara
- TaxJar
- TaxValet
- Vertex

These apps can automate sales tax collection, manage state reporting requirements, and file state sales tax returns. They scale along with your business, so you won't have to worry about switching providers as your sales grow.

NEVER MESS WITH PAYROLL TAXES

Warning! Trouble Ahead!

The Tax Division of the US Department of Justice (DOJ) pays special attention to payroll taxes. Employers are legally responsible for collecting taxes from employees and submitting that money to the IRS. When that doesn't happen, the DOJ can (and will) pursue civil and criminal investigations often resulting in huge financial penalties and possibly jail time.

UNDERSTANDING THE DIFFERENT TYPES OF PAYROLL TAXES

Payroll taxes can be sorted into two main categories: employee withholding taxes and employer taxes. Withholding taxes are deducted from employee pay—you've probably seen that on your paychecks. Employer taxes are in addition to employee pay, increasing the overall payroll-related expenses. Both categories include federal and state taxes. Withholding taxes include federal income tax, state income tax, Social Security, and Medicare.

Employer taxes include a matching contribution to Social Security and Medicare, collectively known as FICA (Federal Insurance Contributions Act), and federal and state unemployment taxes.

TRUST FUND TAXES

Employee withholding taxes are also known as trust fund taxes. That's because as the employer, you're entrusted to collect and remit those taxes on behalf of your employees. It's the amount taken out of their paychecks for taxes—it's their money, not the company's.

When you don't remit those withholding taxes, you are technically stealing money from your employees. That's why the DOJ and the IRS takes this so seriously and the punishments are so severe. Anyone involved in the company payroll could be at risk of consequences, including the company itself, owners, and the bookkeeper who processes payroll.

UNPAID PAYROLL TAX PENALTIES

The IRS and DOJ have a lot of options for punishing companies that have not collected payroll taxes. It's a very serious crime, so some of the potential forms of discipline are:

- Fines
- Interest on unpaid back taxes
- Property liens
- Jail sentences
- Other civil or criminal sanctions (like probation, for example)

The fines imposed depend on a number of factors, including the size of the company, whether payments were late or never made, and how late payments were remitted. The later the payment, the bigger the fine, ranging from 2% if the payment is no more than five days late to 15% if it's more than ten days since the IRS sent a notice.

With the steep punishments the government doles out, you can see why it's so important to comply with all payroll tax regulations and never skip or skimp on payroll tax payments. But it happens much more than you'd think.

A Billion Dollar Problem

According to the DOJ Tax Division, unpaid payroll taxes are an enormous problem. Withholding taxes make up around 70% of all the money collected by the IRS. Unpaid payroll taxes amount to $79 billion of the US net tax gap, the portion of unpaid taxes the IRS expects to never be able to collect.

WHY WOULDN'T I MAKE TAX PAYMENTS?

Small business owners often struggle with cash flow, and that can lead to some desperate decision-making. They try to delay any payments they can just to stay afloat. Payroll usually ranks among the highest business expenses, with payroll taxes making up a hefty chunk of that. In these cases, tax payments are seen as a luxury—a problem for the future.

Payroll taxes, especially for small businesses, may not need to be paid as often as employee wages. They're also easier to skip than other expenses that have an immediate impact on the business, like rent and paying employees. Prioritizing these everyday expenses can lead business owners to use tax funds, expecting to be able to find the money before they run into trouble. When they can't come up with the money, they may delay filing payroll tax returns and remitting the amount due or skip it entirely. This is not the right way to deal with company cash flow problems, and the IRS doesn't consider not having enough money as a reasonable excuse for nonpayment or late payment.

Using a payroll service can help avoid this issue, as most of these services withdraw tax payments for each payroll and hold them until it's time to remit. That doesn't solve the company cash flow problem, but it will keep the feds off your back for unpaid payroll taxes.

There are some circumstances where the government won't impose penalties on unreported taxes or late payments (such as natural disasters, fires, serious illness, death, or a legitimate inability to access records).

Any reasonable excuse will need to be backed up by documentation, such as proof of damage and an insurance claim in the case of a fire, or a doctor's note or hospital record in the case of a severe illness, in order for the government to remove penalties.

STATES IMPOSE PENALTIES TOO

Most states require that income taxes be withheld from employee pay then reported and remitted by the employer just like federal withholding taxes. And state governments will also penalize you for not filing and not paying payroll taxes.

The rules, of course, vary from state to state, but virtually all of them have a list of potential penalties related to payroll taxes, along with interest on the back taxes. For example, New York penalizes employers who don't pay on time, who don't file online, and who don't use the correct filing format.

HOW TO KEEP YOUR TAX PREPARER HAPPY

Don't Chuck Responsibilities Into the "Later" Pile

One of the key reasons for keeping timely and accurate books is tax reporting. Your tax preparer can't even begin to work on your personal or company's tax return without clean year-end financial statements. These statements require all transactions for the year to have been recorded and properly categorized, for all accounts to be reconciled, and all relevant receipts to be scanned for electronic storage.

If you want your business's (and your own) tax returns completed on time, you'll need to provide all of that information to your tax preparer at least six weeks ahead of the due date. If your records are incorrect or incomplete, your tax preparer will not be able to work on the returns. This can be especially problematic for pass-through entities like partnerships and S corporations, as the business owners won't be able to file their personal tax returns without information from the business tax return.

FINALIZE THE YEAR-END BOOKKEEPING

The first thing your tax pro will need is current, correct financial statements for the business, typically including at least a P&L and a balance sheet. If your books aren't up-to-date and have a lot of unprocessed transactions, you'll have to get them caught up before submitting them for tax preparation. In addition to processing transactions, you'll want to review every account to make sure the numbers/finances are close to what you expected. Account balances that look off to you probably have been calculated incorrectly, and those need to be fixed before your taxes can get done. For example, if you know you paid employee salaries of $60,000, but the salary expense account balance is $94,250, you can see that something has been miscategorized.

You also want to make sure that any expenses you've paid with personal funds, like with your credit card, get added into the books if you haven't already reimbursed yourself. Those will either go on the books as owner contributions or loans from the owner, depending on how your accountant recommends handling them. It's important to include these expenses so you can see how much it really costs to run your business, and so that you don't overpay taxes on business income. Once all of the numbers look right, you can get on with the next step: reconciling accounts.

Confused about Categories?

When you have transactions that you're not sure how to handle, contact your tax person to ask how to categorize them. For example, you might not be sure whether worker's compensation goes under payroll expenses or insurance, or if meals you pay for while traveling go in the same category as client dinners, so check in with your tax preparer. If you handle it right away, it will make it much easier to discuss the transactions, rather than trying to figure it out months later.

RECONCILE YOUR ACCOUNTS

One key step in ensuring the accuracy of your accounting records is reconciling accounts. Reconciling accounts means making sure that the account balance in your bookkeeping matches an outside source, like a bank statement. Sometimes transactions get overlooked in your bookkeeping, or sometimes statements contain mistakes. Matching your accounts to outside sources every month helps you make sure both the books and the statement are accurate. When they're not, figuring out the mismatch lets you correct any problems in your bookkeeping or alert the outside source that there's an error on their side.

When it's an outside error, time matters. Many banks and credit card companies, for example, give you sixty days to report mistakes. Past that deadline, they may not fix the problem, and if the problem at hand involves refunding money to your business, you may lose out if you don't handle it swiftly.

It may seem obvious, but the accounts that should be reconciled deal with the day-to-day financial aspects of your business. The accounts to look at include:

- Bank accounts
- Investment accounts
- Credit card accounts
- Loans
- Payment platforms like PayPal and Square
- Payroll
- Payroll taxes

Most bookkeeping software has some type of reconciliation function. You can also create your own manual bank reconciliation (also called "bank rec") in a spreadsheet. The most important thing to remember is reconciling relevant accounts monthly will save your business a lot of potential headaches down the line. It's easier to figure out and correct one month's worth of mismatches than a whole year all at once. And if your accounts are not reconciled, your tax preparer won't be able to rely on the information you provide them, which typically results in a higher tax prep bill for you.

HOW TO SHARE RECEIPTS

This is not a comedy movie: Your tax preparer does not want a shoebox full of paper receipts. They also don't want photos of receipts, regardless of the format. What they do want: PDFs of major receipts. Keep in mind that what qualifies as a major receipt may vary depending on your preparer's threshold. For example, they don't need seventy-five gas receipts for $60 each. But they probably do need the receipt for the new laptop you bought for $2,200.

Most tax preparers have portals where you can upload your information. This allows them to view and organize the files more easily. So, if your preparer has a portal, use it. Do not send receipts as attachments to emails, especially if you have a great deal of receipts to send over.

Some bookkeeping software allows you to attach PDF receipts directly to transactions. If your tax preparer has access to your books, they'll be able to see the receipts there, and you won't need to upload them anywhere else. This is a great example of how setting yourself up and organizing early helps with headaches down the line.

AVOID THESE COMMON PROBLEMS

Accountants and tax preparers who work with small business owners tend to see the same issues crop up over and over again. Some of them can be easily fixed or adjusted at year-end, but others can be tricky to deal with. Check in with your accountant during the year to make sure you're handling financials correctly, which can help you avoid tax complications at year-end. Some of the most common tax-related problems include:

- Paying yourself the wrong way.
- Mixing business and personal finances.
- Not tracking mileage when you use your personal car for the business.
- Not making estimated tax payments during the year.
- Forgetting to include start-up expenses before your business was officially launched.

Communicating with your accountant or tax preparer from the time you start your business can keep you from making expensive mistakes. Plus, keeping those lines open during the year with periodic check-ins can help you make sure your books are being kept properly. When you're on top of your finances, your business has a much higher ability to grow!

Chapter 7

Your Business and Your Life

When you're building a business, it may feel like your business and your life are one and the same. Keeping them separate as much as possible will protect both, but it's tough to keep them from overlapping, especially during a crisis—whether it's a natural disaster or the loss of your biggest customer. Planning distinct business and personal time and preparing for emergencies in advance can help make sure you're participating in both aspects of your life, leading to a better quality of life and less risk of burnout.

As your business grows, so will your time commitment. While overnight success seems like a great idea, a slow and steady growth pace is more realistic and sustainable. Thinking now about how you'll eventually want to wind down your business, whether that means closing up shop entirely or handing the reins over to someone else, gives you time to make the smoothest possible exit. And when you're finally ready to be done with this chapter, you'll be able to transition to your new life without sacrificing all that you've worked for.

PREPARING FOR A BUSINESS CRISIS

Batten Down the Hatches

From global issues like pandemics to losing inventory in a fire to getting slammed by a hurricane, all kinds of crises can crop up at any time—whether you're ready for them or not. The trick to surviving these crises is to have a plan in place for any likely issues that crop up for your business. You can't anticipate everything, of course, but some more common issues can be planned for before they cause your business to go under.

Natural disasters have become frighteningly common, and they cause up to billions in business losses. Recession and inflation may not count as "disasters" per se, but they can be disastrous for small businesses. Each of these things can be prepared for in its own way.

KNOW WHAT YOUR INSURANCE COVERS

Small businesses (even micro-sized businesses with only one employee) need insurance. Insurance will protect the company against total loss in the event of a natural crisis. Without it, the business will need to fund its own recovery, shelling out cash to replace lost assets or repair damaged ones. Insurance helps protect the key physical elements of your business.

That said, as important as insurance is, it's equally important to know exactly what your insurance policy covers. You may be surprised by how many common occurrences are specifically excluded from your insurance plan unless you pay extra. For example, flooding typically requires separate coverage no matter where your business is located. Don't wait until you need to file a claim to review your policy because by then it will be too late to get any missing coverage.

While everything is fine, make sure to clearly document all of your company's assets. Physical assets can be catalogued and photographed so you have definite proof of their existence pre-disaster. Keep these records with your insurance policy so you'll know exactly where they are when you need them. You will want to keep these assets in an easily accessible location and preferably online—if you keep them as physical documents, they may not be recoverable during a crisis.

If your business faces a higher-than-average risk of disaster damage, a separate business interruption insurance policy (which helps replace income lost while your business is temporarily shut down due to emergency) may be worth investigating. Consider working with a trusted insurance broker, one who works and gets paid by multiple insurance companies, to help you navigate your insurance needs, understand current policies, and file claims when disaster strikes.

CREATE A BUSINESS CONTINUITY PLAN

When you're smack in the middle of a disaster, it's impossible to figure out next steps on the fly. That's why it's important to create a business continuity plan while things are calm. This type of plan details how your company will operate during and after a disaster, with clear and specific steps to take. To create an effective plan, you'll need to think through how various crises will impact your company, its resources, and its ability to operate. You can find detailed information, tools, checklists, and sample plans in the Ready Business section on the US government website www.ready.gov.

A thorough business continuity plan will include:

- An emergency budget.
- A continuity leader or team to implement the plan.
- A way to protect and preserve vital company records.
- Details on how to set up cybersecurity protocols for recordkeeping and network access.
- A way to set employees up to be able to work remotely.
- A plan to locate backup production facilities.
- Details on how to find alternate suppliers.

Once you've written up the plan, the continuity team will practice it. Running simulations and springing surprise tests on the team will help ensure they're ready to handle an actual disaster if or when it occurs.

Natural Disasters Damage Small Businesses

According to the most recent *Small Business Credit Survey* conducted in 2021, one in ten small businesses with employees experienced loss from a natural disaster within the prior year. And 38% of those businesses had been previously affected by a similar disaster. This shows how important it is to have a plan in place before a crisis occurs.

DEALING WITH FINANCIAL CRISIS

When the economy is flailing, your business will be affected. At some point you'll have to deal with recession, inflation, or supply chain issues. Any of those factors could tank your business if you aren't prepared. While you may feel limited in what your small company can do in the face of economic turmoil, there are actions you can take now that will make it easier to ride out whatever's going on in the economy as a whole.

First step: Create a business emergency savings fund. These are just as important for businesses as they are for people, and they can help you avoid dipping into your personal emergency account. Ideally, it will hold about 3–6 months' worth of essential operating expenses: the absolute bare necessities needed to run the company. Insurance payouts and disaster loans can take time to receive, often more time than you have. Especially during a crisis, access to cash can mean the difference between survival and total loss.

Second step: Plan ahead for liquidity. Take stock of all of your potential cash resources, and regularly update them. Foster good relationships with the banks your business uses, particularly with any loan managers, whenever possible. Keep communications open with investors and partners who don't deal with the day to day. Get business credit cards and use them sparingly while not in a crisis, as those can give you some breathing room during a cash crunch. Consider applying for a business line of credit when you don't need it. You're more likely to be approved when you're in a good position rather than when your company is flailing.

Third step: Take defensive actions. If you have only one big customer providing most of your revenues, look for a few more to spread out your company's earning capabilities. Look into other suppliers who may offer better prices or terms that may not have been available to your business previously, or may have access to different product pipelines than your current suppliers. Get in the habit of promptly collecting payment from your customers rather than letting them slide. When possible, switch to prepayment or subscription-based payment models to make incoming cash flow more predictable.

MANAGING CHANGE

Turning with the Tides

The world changes faster than ever, and your business has to be able to keep up. Adaptability, flexibility, and preparedness will help your company meet challenges without falling apart. You'll have to deal with things like new technologies, shifting customer demands and interests, and losing key employees—those are all predictable occurrences, though the timing can come as a surprise. Wholly unexpected challenges could crop up as well, like Covid-19, that will send shockwaves through every part of your life and business.

If your business can't navigate change, it will fail. But just like collecting food supplies and toilet paper prior to a blizzard, there is a lot you can do ahead of time to help face these transitions. Of course, it's impossible to foresee and prepare for everything that might happen. So, having at least a vague plan to handle common challenges and changes will help keep your business running for years to come.

TECHNOLOGY CHANGES CONSTANTLY

For the average, non-tech-oriented person, technology can be hard to keep up with. Software, apps, platforms, and hardware change quickly, and the ones you're used to can become obsolete in no time flat. The sheer number of options for new tech can be overwhelming, so it's important to understand what your business actually needs to stay current and competitive. The right tech can expand opportunities and improve your business. The wrong tech wastes time and money, two valuable resources you can't afford to squander. Before you invest in technology, figure out exactly what you need and why. At the very least you'll need a computer or tablet, a phone, a website, and the right mix of software and apps to get your business up and running.

Some commonly needed software and apps for small businesses are:

- Customer relationship management (CRM)
- Payment processing
- Sales and invoicing
- Cybersecurity solutions
- Online data storage
- Accounting/bookkeeping
- Project management
- Scheduling calendar
- Video communication
- Social media
- Inventory management/POS

It's important to update software, apps, and operating systems as soon as updates become available. Updates generally improve the security, efficiency, and effectiveness of the technology. Ignoring or skipping them can cause problems with integrated apps, time lags, and insecure data. Keeping up with tech trends for your industry can keep you current and help you figure out what trends your business needs to follow.

CHANGING CUSTOMER DEMANDS

What do customers want? This is one of the trickiest things to figure out, and once you have, it often changes. With constant instant access, personalized in-person and online shopping experiences, and free delivery, customers are in control of where they shop and what they buy. They can compare prices in just a few clicks and make purchase decisions in seconds flat. Getting to know your target customers inside and out and encouraging communication with them will keep you on the inside track as their wants and needs change.

It can be difficult for small businesses to compete on things like price, so building trust with your customers and delivering consistently excellent customer service are essential. Your company philosophy, core beliefs, and values also matter to customers now more than ever. According to the *Consumer Culture Report*, 71% of consumers want to buy from companies that share their values.

Fostering two-way relationships with your customers is essential to keeping them and attracting new customers in the same target market. You communicate with them through your website, email marketing, and social media. It's at least equally important to hear from them and ask them what they want and what could make their customer experience better. You can get more information from your customers by:

- Encouraging engagement on social media.
- Sending out customer surveys and questionnaires.
- Keeping track of customer service issues and addressing them promptly.
- Asking them directly what new product features, products, and services they want.
- Inviting them to test new products and services.

As you're learning about your customer base's changing demands, you'll also be building up their trust and loyalty. Customers that feel cared about and listened to will stick around, even if you can't always match the competition's prices.

LOSING A KEY EMPLOYEE

Your employees rank among your company's most important assets, all of them adding value to the business. There are some employees, though, that become crucial for your business success. And when they leave, they can leave gaping holes in the business. It can feel like a catastrophe, but you can take steps now to make any transitional period easier. This is especially important when that employee does things that no one else on staff knows how to do or has created their own system for getting things done.

Step 1: Assess their role, their skills, and their knowledge set. Create a detailed job description based on what this employee does and how they do it.

Step 2: Document systems, workflows, and processes for the job so that someone else could jump in if necessary.

Step 3: Teach other employees different pieces of the key employee's job, spreading out the knowledge and skills as much as possible.

Step 4: Keep an eye open for replacement talent should the need arise. Connect with recruiters, have a job post ready to go, and connect with your network even though you don't have an open position right now. When you do, you'll be ready and able to fill it quickly.

Time Off Matters Too

Your key employee needs backup even if they're not quitting. Their work needs to get done if they're out on leave or tied up on a project. Inviting them to explain their process so they don't have to deal with a huge backlog can incentivize them to help create the description and train other employees without causing anxiety or fear of job loss.

CHANGES FROM OUT OF THE BLUE

Virtually no one was ready for the seismic impact of the Covid-19 pandemic and its effects on the world as a whole. Around 43% of small businesses closed, at least temporarily, during the first stages of the pandemic (according to a study published in the *Proceedings of the National Academy of Sciences*). Many of those that were able to stay open had written business plans and had cash reserves or resources, as well as the ability to pivot to accommodate the situation.

While there's no way of knowing if a major disruptive force will affect your business, it's still good to have an idea of how you'd handle a major change. For example, many restaurants survived by switching to pick-up only. Therapists, coaches, and other personal service providers began offering online sessions. Whatever kind of business you have, there will be a way forward in almost any circumstance as long as you've prepared for potential changes.

SETTING BOUNDARIES WITH CUSTOMERS

Don't Let Them Cross the Line

You may not think about business boundaries, but you've respected and dealt with them your whole life. Some common boundaries are as follows: posted hours of operation; no shoes, no shirt, no service signs; notices for doctors who aren't accepting new patients; and no food allowed in the store. For different types of companies, different boundaries will apply.

It will take careful thought and possibly (but hopefully not) some negative experiences to figure out the right boundaries to set for your customers. Any customer who refuses to respect your boundaries is not a good fit for your business.

COMMUNICATING BASIC BOUNDARIES

Your customers and potential customers should be aware of your company's most basic boundaries before they interact with you. Operating hours should be clearly posted on your website or in your business establishment (if you have a physical space for your customers to shop). Contact information should be limited to the ways you want customers to reach out to your business.

Other examples of basic boundaries are:

- Masking requirements (if you work with the elderly, for example).
- Dress requirements (no open footwear in a gym).
- What can and can't be brought in (no outside food in a restaurant, but bring your own wine).

These examples will help you figure out what kind of limits you want to set for your business. Clear and constant communication of these boundaries will make it easier for customers to follow them.

KNOW WHEN TO SAY NO

The very first boundary you'll set with customers involves whether you want to work with them. This is more of an issue for service businesses but can also affect companies that sell products to a limited number of select customers. When either you don't feel comfortable with a potential customer for any reason or don't have the capacity to work with them, politely declining the sale can be your best option. It may feel uncomfortable, but that discomfort will be momentary compared to working with them.

You also have the right to walk away from any customer relationship that's not serving your business. If a customer begins to take advantage by renegotiating prices after work has begun, for example, you can insist on sticking with the original agreement. Valuing yourself and your company by refusing to let bad customers take advantage of your business allows you to have relationships with better clientele.

IMPORTANCE OF WRITTEN CONTRACTS

When your business relies on agreements, whether it's a sales contract to deliver a dozen tractors or an engagement letter for creating a social media marketing campaign, it's important to include every detail you can think of and proactively deal with any potential issues.

Set clear expectations from the start, and repeat them to make sure they sink in. During your initial contact with the customer, explain exactly what they can expect from this transaction. Set expectations regarding price, delivery date, product or service (and provide a thorough description), additional charges for add-ons or changes, and any other relevant terms or conditions.

APPROPRIATE CONTACT

Setting up a business phone and email creates another customer boundary, preventing them from contacting you personally. And unless you take on customers at your home (such as in a home office for a consultation), do not give out your home address. Make sure your customers can easily find the appropriate ways to contact you on your website, invoices, and business cards. Any contact method that you have not provided is not appropriate for customers to use.

So if a customer calls or texts your personal phone, sends mail to your home, or shows up to your personal and private property uninvited, they have crossed a significant boundary. Don't let this slide, or it will continue to happen. On the next business day, communicate clearly and politely that you only accept business communications through business channels, and list all the appropriate ways the customer can contact you. Should they violate this boundary again, consider cutting them off in favor of better customers.

NOTHING SHOULD MAKE YOU UNCOMFORTABLE

No customer has the right to make you or your staff feel uncomfortable, threatened, or disrespected. Respectful customers will not degrade you or invade your personal space.

When you're dealing with a rude or upsetting customer, it can be hard not to react emotionally. But strategically, it's better to try to remain calm, professional, and polite. While these attacks feel personal, they're not. They reflect on the customer, not on you, your team, or your company. Remove the disruptive customer from the scene, do your best to listen to what they're saying, and then respond with positive language. This can often defuse, de-escalate, and end the situation. Once things have calmed down, take active steps to ban them to avoid a repeat scenario.

CREATE BOUNDARIES FOR YOUR TEAM

In addition to setting boundaries for customers, it's important to create guidance for customer interactions for you and your team. For example: Avoid sharing personal information (a home address) with individual customers. You also need to reinforce physical boundaries appropriate for the business (give a handshake, not a hug). Be kind, polite, patient, and respectful with your customers, but keep interactions with them during work hours when possible. Finally, discourage inappropriate customer behaviors, and encourage employees to report any harassment immediately.

MAINTAINING WORK-LIFE BALANCE

All Work and No Play

Starting and running a business can take over your life. When you're working to build a company, it demands an excessive amount of time, attention, and energy. Even when you're not at work, you'll be thinking about it unless you make sure to shut down all things business during your personal time. And it is critical to carve out personal nonwork time, whatever that means to you.

One of the biggest issues facing entrepreneurs is burnout. They work so much that there's little time for anything else, and that can lead to long-term stress that eventually causes extreme levels of exhaustion. They ignore physical and mental health issues, torpedo their social lives, and sacrifice family relationships and friendships, all of which can negatively impact their quality of life. Before you sign on for a grind, *don't*. Preserving your work-life balance will keep you sane and help you contribute more to both your business and your personal life.

WHAT EXACTLY IS BURNOUT?

Burnout is a form of work-related chronic stress that frequently affects entrepreneurs, especially when they're starting new companies. The constant drive to get things done at the expense of everything else can lead to health problems for you and your business. Some regular signs of burnout are low or no motivation, irritability, low energy, and physical or emotional exhaustion.

There will always be more that you could be doing to optimize the business. And when you're bootstrapping, all (or most) of the financial, optimization, or structural responsibility falls on your shoulders. But if you don't take care of yourself—if you're not eating well, getting sufficient sleep, and connecting with the people who are important to you—you're setting yourself up for a crash. Though it doesn't seem fair, the business can crash with you.

Most Entrepreneurs Live with Mental Health Issues

According to a study conducted by researchers at UC Berkeley, 72% of entrepreneurs struggle with some form of mental health issues. Of those, 63% report dealing with burnout and 59% with anxiety. Top stressors include financial worries, daily stress, and work-life balance.

SETTING PERSONAL PRIORITIES

Your business will gobble up your whole life if you let it. You can avoid burnout and its inevitable toll by proactively taking steps to enjoy time outside of work. Reconnect with passions you deprioritized when you switched your focus to the business. Get outdoors and get moving. Spend time with your family and friends, walk your dog, or read a book that has nothing to do with business or success. It will certainly get you out of your head and pull your focus from the day job.

Make a list—an actual written list—of people you like being around and activities that bring you joy. Add in things that you do for self-care, like getting a massage, going for a hike, or taking an uninterrupted afternoon nap. Include cultural or sports events, trivia nights, or book club meetings that you'd want to attend if it wouldn't take time away from work. All of these things are personal priorities, and you'll need to make space for them in your life while you're building your business. Missing out on the things that bring you joy and comfort defeats a key purpose of being your own boss, so don't let the business monopolize all your time.

SCHEDULE EVERYTHING

Starting a business takes tons of time, and it's very easy for things to get overlooked or skipped. Creating a detailed schedule will help make sure nothing—including your personal priorities—slips through the cracks. There won't be enough time to get everything done every day, especially in the beginning, so blocking out time for specific tasks will be essential. Time management is key here, so find a system that works for you and use it consistently.

Types of tools you'll want to consider include time trackers, habit trackers, note-taking apps, task or project managers, and scheduling apps. Popular time and project management tools include Asana, Todoist, Trello, TimeCamp, Pomodoro Timer, Evernote, and ClickUp. You'll also want to enlist a calendar app like Calendly or Google Calendar to schedule meetings, appointments, and time blocks.

It may take a while to find the right set of tools for you and your business, so try out a bunch of them to see which feels best for you. Time management will be a critical component of your business success and your ability to avoid burnout.

INVOLVE YOUR FAMILY IN YOUR BUSINESS

One of the biggest pieces of work-life balance is spending time with family. Missed meals, late school pick-up, and skipping date night can take a toll on these important relationships, adding even more stress to your life. The solution is to designate family time: Schedule it and stick to the schedule no matter what's going on in the business.

You may also include your family in your business by sharing new products with them, giving your kids age-appropriate jobs complete with paychecks, or asking for your partner's input in their area of expertise. Keeping them involved helps minimize resentment and frustration, and it also maximizes the time you spend together.

It's equally important to communicate clear boundaries for family time versus work time. Your family doesn't want work to interfere in their time with you, but you need to have strictly work time where you can focus all of your energy and attention on the business.

These boundaries can be especially important for single parents with home-based businesses. Constant interruption can break your flow, making it much harder to get work done in a reasonable amount of time. Set specific work blocks for yourself and create do-not-disturb zones, like your office, to set clear work-time boundaries for your family.

PLANNING FOR SUSTAINABLE GROWTH

Slow and Steady Wins the Race

A lot of small businesses grow accidentally and suddenly. Without preparation, they can't keep up with the new demands and often run out of cash or time, leading to disappointed customers and setbacks. Planning for growth allows your business to expand at a comfortable pace, where you can meet additional demand.

In the beginning, it can be hard to see growth and even harder to sustain it. Putting together a focused plan that includes measurable steps and proven strategies will help your company grow in the way you want it to.

HOW DO YOU MEASURE GROWTH?

In order to see how your company is growing, you need to have a starting point to measure against. You can evaluate your business using specific objective metrics and KPIs (key performance indicators), then choose a time period to re-evaluate those same numbers for comparison. Once you have this baseline, you can also use the information to set growth goals for the future. You can use the following metrics to measure growth:

- Staff size
- Total number of customers
- Lost customers
- Market share
- Sales by dollars and volume

- Profitability (profit as a percent of sales)
- Cash balances

KPIs help you see how well your company is meeting performance goals. With KPIs, you can measure conversion rates, lead generation, monthly email signups, website visitors, and accounts receivable aging (how long it takes customers to pay once invoiced).

Tracking these numbers will give you a sense of your company's growth potential. It also highlights areas of strength and weakness, so you'll know where to focus future growth efforts more effectively. As you track these things over time, you will have concrete numbers to measure your growth against and be able to see if you are on-target for your goals.

Losing Customers Thwarts Growth

While you're focused on bringing in new business, remember to continue to provide an excellent experience to the customers you already have. It costs substantially less to keep customers than to attract new ones. Plus, with your existing relationship, they're more likely to buy add-on products and services from you, promoting growth from the inside.

HAVE APPROPRIATE STAFF, PROCESSES, AND SYSTEMS IN PLACE

It's a tricky balance between being ready to grow and being able to meet increasing demand. If you overinvest in staff, inventory, and other areas to accommodate growth that's not there yet, your business can end up in a cash crisis. On the flip side, if demand grows before your company can meet it, your business will lose potential sales, customers, and money. That's why it's so important to plan for growth at a reasonable pace, taking proactive steps so you can avoid having to react to a change you're not ready for.

Creating easily scalable systems and processes will set your company up for sustainable growth. Automating as many repeat tasks as possible makes it easier to scale without disproportionately increasing costs.

Document your systems and processes in detail and include them as part of staff training. This will help new employees get up to speed quickly, and you will flatten the learning curve. Documenting will also help you refine job descriptions so you can find the right employees for your business—people who will grow with the company and add value. Once you create scalability in your business, you can easily add staff as needed to handle nonautomated functions, rather than hiring on before the company can handle it.

EASING INTO GROWTH

Growing a small business is hard. You have to fight for market share, deal with competitors, and find and connect with the right audience, all while you're serving your regular customers. Try these methods to help you ease into growth in the marketplace.

One great way to quickly increase your reach: Develop strategic partnerships. Basically, you connect with another business that has an overlapping target audience. For example, if your business sells custom picture frames, you could connect with a photographer. The strategic part of the relationship looks different depending on what works for you both. It could be as simple as asking them to mention your business in a post on their website. This mutually beneficial relationship introduces each business to the other's customers in a completely natural way. It's beneficial to both businesses as well as the customers in that space.

Another option: Create lead magnets. These are generally digital products or discount offers that potential customers receive in exchange for their email address or other contact information. The lead magnet generally works as part of a larger sales funnel, encouraging the receiver to take the next step in the buying process. For example, the lead magnet could be a coupon for $10 off a $50 order for first-time buyers. Or it could be a free checklist for students moving into dorms that sends them to an article about the "five best purchases to make dorm living easy" that links to your online shop selling storage containers. Taking steps like these can bring in a manageable number of new customers in a steady stream, rather than all at once.

KEEP AN EYE ON YOUR COMPETITION

Paying attention to your competitors is an important (and often overlooked) piece of the business growth puzzle. It's not enough to just know who your chief competitors are. You also want to track their growth and how they're attracting new business. Are they diversifying and adding new product or service lines? Have they taken over another company? Are they expanding their target audience? You can find out more about your competitor's growth plans by visiting their website, looking at their promotions, and following their social media.

You may gain insights from their choices that you can apply to your growth goals. You may be inspired by their marketing efforts to create a great new campaign for your company. Or, you may find holes in their strategies that your company can fill.

WHEN TO STOP GROWING

Bigger Isn't (Always) Better

As an entrepreneur, you'll constantly be encouraged to grow your business, keep growing, then grow some more. If your goal is to create a company to quickly grow and sell, sort of like flipping houses, that continuous growth pursuit may be your perfect business strategy. But if you're looking to create a business that will support you and your family, provide the products and services your customers need, and give you a sense of personal satisfaction, you might not want to grow beyond your small business.

That doesn't mean you won't welcome new customers or innovate new products and services, and it doesn't mean your business won't continue to grow. What it does mean is that your actions and goals won't be primarily growth-focused, that you'll shift gears toward sustaining what you have instead of chasing what you don't.

WHEN YOU'RE A SOLO ACT

If your business provides personal services that are delivered by you, there's a hard limit on your time. That doesn't mean your business won't have capacity for growth. You can sell your time and experience in different ways, such as online courses or group services, or hiring other qualified professionals to take on new customers, for example. You can grow revenues by judiciously increasing prices or offering add-on services. But if you like being a solopreneur and like the freedom of running your business your way, you'll want to keep it to a manageable size. Plus, if your business is based on your particular skills and talents, you may not feel comfortable delegating to other people.

The key here is figuring out how many hours you want to work and going backward from there. That sets a boundary for your time contribution to the business. Anything more than that will require staff, contractors, or even partners. If you don't want to bring anyone else into the business, you must determine the ideal growth cap that you don't want the business to grow beyond.

WHEN GROWTH IS TOO RISKY

Actively trying to grow your business comes with a degree of risk that not all small business owners want to take. Once your company is generating enough profits and cash flow to meet your needs, you can choose to stay where you are, rather than investing in additional growth. Remember, in order to successfully grow your business, you need to have the right staff and infrastructure in place to handle the increased demand. That means dipping into your cash reserves, taking out loans, or pursuing new investments to finance the expansion.

In many cases, growing a business requires more physical space, additional physical locations, higher inventory levels, new technology, and more employees. All of those factors will be at least temporary cash and profit drains until they start generating enough revenue to cover the expanded costs. If sales don't grow as expected, your business will be stuck running at a loss, potentially with negative cash flow. If you don't feel that the upside of this growth is worth that risk, it's not. Don't feel pressured to grow beyond your comfort level. Trust your gut.

WHEN GROWTH MEANS
REGULATORY HURDLES

When it comes to business regulations, size often matters. Many regulations kick in based on things like number of employees or gross revenues. In some cases, growing your business may call for changing the number of owners and the business structure, resulting in a new set of rules to follow.

Adding your first employee, for example, calls for new tax IDs, a ton of paperwork, frequent tax filings, workers' compensation insurance, and a lot of recordkeeping. So, growing enough to need even one employee adds regulatory hurdles you'll need to clear.

Federal employment-related regulations include:

- The Pregnant Workers Fairness Act (PWFA), which affects employers with at least fifteen employees.
- The Affordable Care Act (ACA), which requires businesses with fifty or more employees to provide health coverage.
- Consolidated Omnibus Reconciliation Act (COBRA), which requires companies with twenty or more employees to offer a temporary extension of health coverage if that coverage otherwise ends (due to layoffs or divorce, for example).
- The Americans with Disabilities Act (ADA), which affects companies with at least fifteen employees.
- The Family and Medical Leave Act (FMLA), which affects companies with at least fifty employees.

You can find out more about size-based employer regulations on the US Department of Labor website at www.dol.gov. Keep in mind that most states have their *own* sets of employment laws, so check your state website to learn about those regulatory hurdles.

Gross revenue growth can also increase your company's regulatory burdens. For example, partnerships with revenues of more than $250,000 or assets exceeding $1 million have to file extra forms with their business tax returns.

Shifting business entities can also add a higher regulatory burden along with formation costs. Going from a sole proprietorship to an LLC may require filing annual reports, franchise tax returns, and other documents, depending on state laws. Going from a partnership or LLC to a corporation brings on another whole set of rules to follow, including writing by-laws, holding shareholder meetings, and recording all share transfers. Plus, that's only if you keep the corporation private. Going public opens up a can of compliance worms that requires a high level of professional legal and accounting assistance to navigate.

Industry-Specific Regulations

On top of general federal and state business laws, many industries must abide by an additional set of tailored regulations. Such industries include farming, aviation, alcohol sales, and broadcast communications. You can find links to the appropriate agencies on the SBA website at www.sba.gov.

GETTING OUT WHEN YOU'RE READY

Time to Say Goodbye

Choosing to leave, sell, or shut down your business can be an extremely difficult emotional and financial decision. You've devoted your time, energy, and heart to this company, and letting go can be hard. That said, once you've made the decision to change your relationship to the business, your next step will be to figure out how you want to wind down your relationship with the business. You have several options here, such as selling, successorship, maintaining ownership but removing yourself from daily operations, or dissolving the company. Whatever you choose, make sure you do it the right way to avoid any post-company complications.

THE RIGHT TIME TO MOVE ON

The choice to step away from your business may involve a host of personal, professional, and financial reasons. Some of the main reasons people choose to walk away are retirement, an offer to buy the business, family or personal health concerns, burnout, difficulty with finances, or changes in customer base. Whatever your reason for moving on, know that you're making the right choice. And now that the decision is made, you can move on to figuring out how you want to deal with it.

Get an Accurate Valuation

Small business valuations can be calculated using a variety of methods, but most include some combination of asset value and revenue streams (sales over a period of time). While valuing assets tends to be straightforward, the value of revenue streams is more complicated to calculate and usually requires a professional.

DISSOLVING YOUR BUSINESS

In some circumstances, it makes sense to close the business. For example, if revenues rely heavily on your particular skills and talent, your stepping down would essentially end the company. Your business may also be too niche to attract buyers, or you might want to sell off any valuable assets and wind down the rest.

Whatever brought you to your decision, make sure you handle this process properly. If your company is an LLC, partnership, or corporation, you'll need to follow all steps laid out in the founding documents. Even if you're the sole owner, you may be required to hold and record a vote to dissolve, for example.

Most states have detailed regulations and processes to dissolve legally registered companies. In most cases, you'll need to file formal articles of dissolution that certify your intent to close the business. You'll also need to cancel any permits, licenses, and legal agreements (like leases) tied to the business. Other tasks you'll need to attend to will depend but generally include:

- Paying any outstanding payroll and payroll taxes.
- Filing income, sales, and payroll tax returns.

- Paying off all company debts, including amounts owed to vendors and contractors, outstanding loans, and outstanding credit card balances.
- Collecting any money due from customers.
- Closing all business-related accounts.
- Closing out the company books.

You'll also need to keep all of the company bookkeeping and payroll records for at least three years in case of audits, inquiries, or other compliance issues.

SUCCESSION PLANNING

Succession planning involves preparing someone else to take over the business when you're ready to step down or if you become unable to run the company for any reason. It is best to start this process years before it's needed to give your successors time to learn how to lead and function in your role.

While it's most common for succession plans to include family members, they don't have to. Plus, even if you do plan for a family member to take over, you may want to involve existing employees in the ongoing management processes because you may need an entire succession team to fill your shoes. You want to ensure as smooth a transition as possible, so advanced planning and prep will be crucial for the process.

Once you've selected your successor(s), you'll create a tailored training program that allows them to learn all necessary skills, with plenty of time to practice them. You'll want to help the successors develop relationships with key stakeholders: from customers to employees to suppliers. When you're ready to step down, your successor(s) will be ready to step in without making any big waves.

When making the decision to have a successor, there's also a tax component to consider, particularly when the person is related to you. When you're handing over the business, rather than just the reins, it may trigger significant tax implications. You and your family may be subject to gift, estate, and generation-skipping taxes.

It's prudent to involve an estate planning attorney, accountant, and financial advisor, especially for closely held family businesses, to help you minimize the tax bite of any transfer. As with anything else in business, choosing a successor requires care.

SELLING THE BUSINESS

Your business may be worth the world to you, but that doesn't mean it's saleable. Before you start the selling process, you'll need to figure out whether anyone will want to buy. Factors to evaluate are:

- History of profitability: Regardless of actual asset value, buyers won't want a business that's struggling financially.
- Asset value: Current market value of assets, including cash, receivables, and real estate, for example, less any liabilities associated with particular assets, such as a mortgage on the real estate.
- Condition of assets: The state of any physical assets and their remaining useful lives.
- Inventory status: The quality, condition, and amount of inventory on hand.

- Supplier relationships: The number of consistent suppliers that work with the business, delivery and payment terms, and whether those relationships are positive and solid.
- Customer base: The number of customers, how long they've been buying from you, and customer engagement data.
- Location: Whether the company's physical location(s) is desirable and convenient.
- General industry: Strength of the industry, whether it's trending up or down.

All of these will factor into the perceived value of your company. Your current business structure (sole proprietorship or S corporation, for example) will also play an important part in how the business can be legally transferred. Before you begin to search for prospective buyers, make sure you understand what's allowed. If you're not the sole owner, you may be required to offer your share to your co-owners before outsiders, which may make it harder for you to leave.

Good prospective buyers to consider pitching to include employees, competitors, strategic partners, other businesses with complementary products or services, and even your customer base. Just as they're assessing the value of your company, you'll need to assess their ability to make the purchase and run the business. You'll need to address whether: you'll be paid in a lump sum or installments, you're willing to sign a noncompete agreement, and you're open to serving as a consultant during the transition. It's in your best interests to have a team of advisors here, including an attorney, an accountant, and a qualified small business appraiser, as you negotiate the deal to sell your business.

INDEX